D0388733

the church before the watching world

francis a. schaeffer

a practical ecclesiology

inter-varsity press
downers grove, illinois 60515

Second printing,
November 1971

InterVarsity Press
is the book publishing
division of
Inter-Varsity Christian
Fellowship.

ISBN 0-87784-542-5
Library of Congress
Catalog Card
Number: 76-166121

Printed in the
United States of
America

contents

introduction

This book is addressed to 20th-century Christians as they face a very practical problem. As Christians we say we believe in truth and in the practice of truth, and yet we face much untruth in the visible church. The problem is not new; error was present in the early church when councils were held to combat it. It was present in the medieval church until the Reformation reaffirmed the biblical faith. And it is present today.

The biblical teaching is clear. As the bride of Christ, the church is to keep itself pure and faithful. And this involves, as I have pointed out in other places, two principles which seem at first to work against each other: (1) the principle of the practice of the purity of the visible church in regard to doctrine and life and (2) the principle of the practice of an observable love and oneness among *all* true Christians regardless of who and where they are.[1] These two principles are, in turn, based on the character of God himself, for God is holy and God is love. In *The Mark of the Christian* I have developed the implications of the second principle for the visible church. The present book will concentrate on the first principle. More specifically it will focus on doctrinal purity. But both principles, because they are based upon the character of God, must be practiced simultaneously. So while we look closely here at the first principle, we must not forget to practice the second.

The issues involved in the principle of the practice of the purity of the visible church in our day in regard to doctrine and life logically break down into several questions. (1) How has the present impurity in the churches come about and what is it? (2) Why should Christians and churches be concerned with doctrinal purity? (3) How can doctrinal purity in the church be maintained in practice? A chapter will be devoted to each of these questions. An appendix, "Some Absolute Limits," will discuss in a different and perhaps unique fashion for modern man the ways in which the trend toward a lack of doctrinal purity

[1] See especially *The Mark of the Christian* (Inter-Varsity Press, 1970), p. 30; *The Church at the End of the 20th Century* (Inter-Varsity Press, 1970), pp. 53-56 and 71-77; and "The Practice of Truth" in *The God Who Is There* (Inter-Varsity Press, 1968), pp. 168-70. Much in *Death in the City* (Inter-Varsity Press, 1969) is also related to these two principles.

can be recognized before it advances beyond the germinal stage.

Although many of the details of this book are drawn from recent ecclesiastical history in the United States, churches almost everywhere face similar problems in slightly different historic settings. In countries as diverse as Korea, Holland and England, one finds almost exact parallels to the American scene. And it is well for Christians in other countries to have a comprehension of what has occurred in the United States ecclesiastically in the last thirty-five years since, in the shifting balances of world influence, American money and American energy have carried these issues directly from America, in allied forms, to Europe and most of the "missionary" countries of the world. Thus, both the principles and the illustrations given here will, I believe, be valuable to churches in every country.

1

a historical critique of theological liberalism

What is the character and form of modern doctrinal impurity and how did it arise? In every age, of course, the church has faced the problem of doctrinal error. The history of Christendom in the last three hundred years, however, has its own peculiar character. In the course of these three hundred years, there have been a number of important historical changes in the nature of the challenge to the biblical perspective. It is especially important to understand the development of such theology as it moves from what we may term the *old liberalism* to the *new liberalism* (existential theology).

Before we take up the details, however, we must

stress the fact that the reason that we reject liberal theology, old and new, is not that we are opposed to scholarship. Constantly through the years great Bible-believing scholars have engaged in what is usually called lower criticism—the question of what the best biblical text really is. Take, for example, such men as Robert Wilson at Princeton Theological Seminary before the changes which have come in that institution. It is natural that biblical Christians should find textual study important, because, since Scripture is the propositional communication from God to men, obviously, we are interested in the very best text possible. Consequently, Christian scholars have labored through the years in the area of "lower criticism."

"Higher criticism" is quite a different matter. Picking up where lower criticism leaves off, it attempts to determine upon its own subjective basis what is to be accepted and what is to be rejected after the best text has been established. The "new hermeneutic" is a case in point, for here there is no real distinction between text and the interpretation; both are run together.

The real difference between liberalism and biblical Christianity is not a matter of scholarship but a matter of presuppositions. Both the old liberalism and new liberalism operate on a set of presuppositions common to both of them, but different from those of historic, orthodox Christianity.

the birth of liberalism

But how did theological liberalism come about? In

order to understand this, we must go back about 250 years to Germany when German theological liberalism was born. At that particular time the German universities and German intellectuals were moving toward modern naturalism. That is, they were moving away from the concept held by the early scientists (such men as Copernicus, Francis Bacon, Galileo and Newton) who believed in the uniformity of natural causes in a limited system open to reordering by both God and man. And they were moving into the concept of the uniformity of natural causes in a closed system, a concept which makes everything that exists a cosmic machine.

That is, an ideological and philosophical shift was taking place. In the academic disciplines surrounding the faculties of theology, the view of the older science (a science whose concept of the uniformity of natural causes in an open system was completely consistent with biblical thought) was being replaced by what I call modern modern science (a concept which, by the uniformity of natural causes in a closed system, eventually leaves no room for God or a significant man). In the academic world, then, a new view was gradually becoming dominant—a total consensus. The result was that the theological faculties became isolated from the other faculties, and, not being able to stand alone, these faculties capitulated in their theology by accepting the naturalism of the other faculties.

I believe that the reason they capitulated is that their theology was already less than it should have been. By the middle of the eighteenth century in the

German universities, the theology of the Reformation with the burning heart was coming to an end. What there was of orthodox theology had largely become only repetitive. Such a theology, of course, can never stand for long.

In church history a cycle seems to recur: Living orthodoxy moves to dead orthodoxy and then to heterodoxy. It would seem that this was the case in the German universities at that particular time. The German theologians did not accept their own form of naturalism because they were forced to do so by the facts. They did so to conform, and liberal theology has been conforming ever since. For, from that day to this, liberal theology has been a theology of naturalism.

It is interesting, but not surprising, that from the time when theology became naturalistic, it has tended simply to follow the curve of secular naturalism. It really says nothing different from the surrounding consensus—whatever the surrounding non-theological consensus is, theological liberalism has simply conformed to it. If we were to graph the curve of the shifting secular naturalistic consensus in red ink and then were to graph the teaching of liberal theology in green ink, we would find almost identical curves, with the theological liberalism simply following a few years later and using religious terms instead of secular ones. Liberal theology uses different terminology and yet says the same thing just a short time later. It has a naturalistic perspective that is totally opposite from the perspective of historic Christianity and the Bible.

the biblical perspective

Basically, the biblical perspective is this. First, there is an infinite-personal God who exists and who has created the external universe, not as an extension of his own essence, but out of nothing. Something of the nature of this created universe can be found out by reason because that is the way the infinite-personal God has created it.[1] The universe is neither chaotic nor random, but orderly. Cause and effect is real, but this cause and effect is not in a closed system but rather in an open system—or, to say it in a different way, it is a cause-and-effect system in a limited time span. Though this universe has an objective existence apart from God, it does not operate solely on its own: It is not autonomous. God is not a slave to the cause-and-effect world he has created, but is able to act into the cause-and-effect flow of history.

Second, God has made man in his own image, and this means, among other things, that man too can act into the cause-and-effect flow of history. That is, man cannot be reduced to only a part of the machine; he is not an automaton.

Third, God not only can act into the world, but he is not silent; he has spoken to men in the historic, space-time situation. The Bible and Christ in his office of prophet have given a propositional, verbalized communication to men that is true about God, true about history and true about the cosmos. This should not take us by surprise, for if God has made

[1] See *Escape from Reason* (Inter-Varsity Press, 1968), pp. 30-32.

man in his own image and has made us so that we can propositionally verbalize facts to each other on a horizontal level of communication, then it is natural that the infinite God who is personal would also communicate vertically to man in the same way. Of course, we must be careful to make a distinction here. Although God has not given us exhaustive knowledge (only he is infinite), he has given us true knowledge (what I have often called true truth)—true knowledge about himself, about history and about the cosmos.[2]

Fourth, the universe as it is now is not normal; that is, it is not now as it was when it was first created. Likewise, man is no longer as he was when first created. Therefore, from God's side, there is the possibility of a qualitative solution to man as he is now and to man's cruelty, without man ceasing to be man.

We should notice at this point how opposed the biblical perspective is to naturalism (the uniformity of cause and effect in a closed system), for naturalism discounts by presupposition this possibility. It bases its understanding of human life and the form of the universe by presuppositionally shutting itself up to finite man totally starting from himself to gather whatever particulars may be so gathered and then trying to make universals and finding meaning only from himself, while ruling out the possibility of

[2] For a consideration of this at much greater length from a philosophical perspective, considering metaphysics, morals and epistemology, see *He Is There and He Is Not Silent,* to be published by Tyndale House Publishers in the United States and by Hodder and Stoughton in Britain.

knowledge from all other sources. Naturalism leaves no room for miracle and eventually leaves no room for the significance of man.

While there are certainly many more details that could be included in the biblical perspective if one were to make the outline more complete, the present description will suffice for our critique of liberalism here.[3]

the steps to modern naturalism

Historically, in the shift from theological orthodoxy to today's present existential theology, three major steps were taken. The first step I have already indicated: the movement from a belief in the uniformity of natural causes in a system open to reordering by God and man to the concept of the uniformity of natural causes in a closed system. Let us consider this step more fully.

During the period between the Renaissance and Reformation, and the age of Rousseau, Kant, Hegel and Kierkegaard, the mood of the secular thinkers was optimistic. They believed that on the basis of rationalism, man could rationally find a unified answer to all of knowledge and life.

According to *rationalism*, as I am using the term here, man can understand the universe by beginning from himself without any recourse to outside knowledge, specifically outside knowledge or revelation from God. The term, *rationality*, sounds very similar,

---

[3] Those who wish to pursue the subject of the biblical perspective in somewhat more detail may wish to refer at this point to the appendix, "Some Absolute Limits."

but the difference in meaning is profound. *Rationality* means that reason is valid. The first axiom in the classical concept of rational methodology is that "A is not non-A." That is, if a proposition is true, then its opposite is not true. Or, in the area of morality, if a certain thing is right, then its opposite is wrong. One should not, therefore, confuse the terms *rationalism* and *rationality*.

The secular thinkers, then, that we are referring to in this period believed optimistically that they could begin only from themselves (this is rationalism), apply reason (rationality) and come to a unified concept of knowledge and of life. They thought that this would lead them to find true answers. They were optimists at this time on the basis of reason.

Where did liberal theology stand in that same period? As I mentioned, liberal theology simply echoed the surrounding rationalistic consensus. In this period the liberal theologians were also optimistic. They believed on the basis of rationalistic scholarship that they could find the historical Jesus while eliminating the supernatural from the biblical account. They believed that they could take reason, apply it to the Bible, and come up with the historical Jesus while getting rid of the supernatural element they found in the biblical account. By presupposition, they were naturalists, and the supernatural made them uncomfortable. But notice that basically they were simply following exactly that which the secular thinkers had already said. The liberal theology was operating in the more limited area of its own discipline, but within that area it was saying the same thing and it had the same mentality.

the step to despair
What, then, was the second step? This step takes us to
Rousseau, Kant, Hegel and Kierkegaard or Kierke-
gaardianism. At this point the secular rationalistic
philosophers concluded that on a rational basis they
could not find a unified answer to knowledge and to
life. Their quest ended in failure. In other words,
accepting the validity of reason and arguing as
reasonably as they could, basing their arguments only
in rationalism, they finally concluded that they could
not put all the pieces together. Their optimism was
gone.

What, then, happened to liberal theology? Liberal
theology simply followed suit. Liberal theologians
had been optimistic about being able to separate the
historical Jesus from the supernatural elements of the
gospel account, but with Albert Schweitzer's failure
in his book, *The Quest of the Historical Jesus,* they
found that they were not going to be able to do it.
This was the end of an era. They discovered that the
supernatural and the historical Jesus were so united
that if all the supernatural was removed, no historical
Jesus remained. And if one kept the historical Jesus,
some supernatural had to stay. So their end was
failure and their optimism was gone.

the step to modern mysticism
The third step for both the secular and the religious
thinkers is a very interesting one. For after the failure
of rationalism, if one keeps his rationality, there are

two possibilities. The first is to become nihilistic. That is, on the basis of reason, they could have concluded that all is blackness and then given up hope.[4] Their other rational alternative was to conclude that their rationalism was wrong, that men, being finite, cannot gather enough particulars to make up the universals, that, in fact, men need knowledge outside of themselves if they are ever to find a satisfactory answer to life. In other words, it would have been reasonable to accept the possibility of revelation or at least the necessity for revelation. But, of course, to do this they would have to give up their presupposition of rationalism. The point is that they could have taken either of these alternatives and have yet remained men of reason.

It must have been a hard moment for them: They had to choose between these two alternatives if they were going to keep their rationality. Instead, they did something new. They did what previously would have been unthinkable to educated men: They split the field of knowledge. They held onto their rationalism by letting go of the concept of a unified field of knowledge. Philosophers had formerly thought that they would be able to come up with a unity on the basis of reason, but they abandoned this hope.

Rather, they now accepted that on the basis of reason men will always come to pessimism—man is a machine and meaningless. Therefore, they developed a concept of non-reason, an attempt for man to achieve meaning and significance outside the frame-

[4] This problem in epistemology is developed in detail in *He Is There and He Is Not Silent*.

work of rationality. For them, everything which makes human life as human life worth living falls in the area of non-reason, what I call in my other books the upper story.

It is crucial that we understand the situation here. The areas of reason and non-reason are held to be completely apart. Picture the line between reason and non-reason as a solid concrete wall with barbed wire in the middle charged with 10,000 volts of electricity. Then you can begin to understand how there can be no interchange between the lower story with reason which leads to despair and the upper story of hope without reason. Everything that is worthwhile for human life—meaning, values, love, etc.—is always in the area of non-reason. In what we may now call the new humanism we have a semantic mysticism with no facts.

existential theology

How does liberal theology fit into this? Liberal theology makes the same shift as secular naturalism. Karl Barth and his disciples, and the theology that sprang up out of the Lutheran world at the University of Lund, Sweden, developed what has come to be called transcendental theology, neo-orthodoxy, or existential theology. Karl Barth, however, is basically the originator of the movement, and it will be sufficient to concentrate on his contribution.

First, one must realize that to the end of his life he continued to accept the higher critical theories. Thus for him there were many mistakes in the Bible. Some have said that Karl Barth's contribution was to sound a bell in the midst of this century's great need for authority. What he really did was give liberal theology a peg in midair. To put it simply, he tried the impossible feat of producing an authority while accepting the results and techniques of higher criticism. To Karl Barth and his followers a statement in the Bible can be historically false and yet religiously true. It was a very simple step but entirely revolutionary. With it theology stepped from the solid earth of rationality into a land where anything can happen.

Karl Barth's basic position was this: Of course, the Bible has all kinds of mistakes in it, but it doesn't matter; believe it religiously. In his first *Römerbrief* (1919) he indicated his relationship to Kierkegaard, and in his *Dogmatics,* II, it is plain that Karl Barth is an existentialist as far as epistemology is concerned.

At the end of his life Barth struggled to hold back the natural direction which he had opened to a man like Tillich and to the death-of-God theology which followed. He did not like what was produced; nevertheless, he was the one who opened the door.

The older liberalism was a heresy from a Christian viewpoint, but from a classical, philosophical viewpoint, it was respectable. The older liberalism was demonstrated most clearly perhaps by a man like Harry Emerson Fosdick in the United States. He and others like him gradually spun a rosy idealism which overlooked the world as it is, but they stayed within the circle of thought wherein one man says, "What I say is true," and another man if he holds the opposite says, "No, your view is false and mine is true." They changed the definition of words so that their terminology needed a whole new series of definitions, but at least when one understood their definitions there was a certain stability in the matter.

But the newer liberals, the existential theologians, do not define their terms so clearly, and, furthermore, they want to say that two mutually contradictory statements may very well both be true. In a very real sense this theology is the child of Hegel. Hegel taught that a *thesis* naturally leads to an *antithesis* and these together lead to a *synthesis.* (To come to this conclusion, one sets aside the methodology of antithesis.) But even this synthesis is only relative, for it too generates its own antithesis, then further synthesis and so on ad infinitum.

The new liberals, therefore, often say *both-and* to two mutually exclusive propositions. One example is saying that Christ both rose physically from the dead and that he did not rise physically from the dead. This is not just a modern problem of semantics. For example, some of the most far out Roman Catholic progressive theologians at the World Congress on the Future of the Church who met in Brussels in September 1970 insisted that they believed in the bodily resurrection of Jesus yet also said that, if one had been there that day, this event could not have been verified by the use of normal means of verification. This is understandable in the context of the *both-and* mentality Or, to say it another way, the bodily resurrection is an upper-story matter.

I remember hearing a certain existential theologian some years ago. After he had finished, I overheard one old Christian saying to another, "Wasn't it wonderful?" The other answered, "It was wonderful, but I couldn't understand it." True Christianity is quite different. When the Bible says, "In the beginning God created the heavens and the earth," a child and a philosopher can understand that it means God created the heavens and the earth in antithesis to the idea that God did not create the heavens and the earth. It does not mean that we can plumb to the exhaustive depths of all God knows about this, but it does mean that the basic facts have been clearly expressed in antithesis to the opposite. With the paradox-ridden new liberal theology, statements have a way of seeming to be profound while actually being only vague. To get the full impact of this, just read a chapter in the works of B. B. Warfield, J. Gresham Machen, Abraham Kuyper, Martin Luther or John Calvin, and then read a chapter by one of the existential theologians.

Let me take another illustration. One of the clearest expressions of the *both-and* type of thinking came to me when a pastor raised on this theology said to me, "The classical Roman Catholic priest is closer to you than I am." When I asked him what he meant, he said, "The priest holding the historic Roman Catholic position and you at least agree that one is right and one is wrong. But we say you are both right." In other words as far as "religious truths" are concerned to this man, it is proper, for example, to say *both* that Christ is the only mediator between God and man *and* at the same time that Mary and the saints intercede for us.

While I was in Finland some years ago, a Bible-believing university professor there used the following illustration. A new liberal, he says, is like a shop-keeper who keeps many things under the counter. When the old-fashioned liberal comes in and asks for old-fashioned liberalism, the new liberal reaches under the counter and says, "That is *just* what we have here." When the Bible-believing Christian comes in, the new liberal reaches under the counter and says, "That is *just* what we have here." The new theology is able to do this because of its *both-and* mentality. Opposites can still be religiously true.

Take, for example, the concept of the Fall. The old liberal, in casting aside the fact of man's sinfulness as taught in the Bible, built for himself an idealistic world that didn't exist. The utopia built by man was to arrive tomorrow. The new liberal, a man like Reinhold Niebuhr, for example, says that man is very deeply flawed (he may even use the word *sinner* to describe this), and therefore he seems closer to the true world than the old-fashioned liberal. But how did man get to be a sinner and what *is* sin? The Bible tells us that man fell in the Garden of Eden. The new liberal says that it does not matter if historically there ever was a Garden of Eden; he tries to lay hold of the realism that man is cruel while dispensing with the Bible's explanation of how he became this way. Thus he hangs his peg in midair, casting aside the histor-icity of the Scripture and yet trying to retain the results that the Bible teaches.

In the matter of individual doctrines, this leads the new liberal into many strange places. The upshot of this position is that there is no clear line between God the Father and God the Son, no clear line concerning the deity of Christ, no clear line between Christ and the sinfulness of man or between what Christ did for us and what happens to us personally. We are told that the really important thing is what happens to us now.

Furthermore, there is no clear line between a lost man and a saved man. With the loss of antithesis there is an implicit or explicit universalism in the new liberalism. One existential theologian in Holland told me in a conversation that the division among men is not vertical but horizontal. When I asked him what he meant, he said that it is not that some men are justified before God and some are not, but that all men are right and all men are wrong. Of course, no Christian is perfect, but by his terminology and in our talk it was clear that this was not what he meant.

Hence, the existential theologian speaks to the world as though the world were the church and to the church as though it were the world. There never is a clear line, because any real concept of antithesis is foreign to him.

It is curious that way back in the summer of 1949, Dr. Hedeinus, an atheistic professor of philosophy at the University of Uppsala, Sweden, wrote a book in which he criticized the theological professors at Lund, accusing them of being "atheists, clothed as bishops and pastors." He further commented that if Christianity is something reasonable that an intelligent man can believe, it should be able to be put into words that can be understood. In short, he said, If the new liberalism is Christianity, I do not want it; its concepts cannot even be put into understandable words, and it is in a worse position than I am. This, of course, is exactly what much later J. S. Bezzant said in *Objections to Christian Belief* when he called this type of theology nonsense.[5]

the bible and the word of God

I have emphasized that there are no clear doctrinal lines in the new theology, but I must make one exception. The new liberals do raise a definite chorus that the Bible is *not* the Word of God. Their well-known words are, "The Bible is not the Word of God, but contains the Word of God." Protestantism has historically centered its authority in the Bible. But the new liberals, although they have cut loose from this, still act as if they have an authority. It is as though a man had torn down a bridge and then walked across the thin air as if the bridge were still there.

In theory the new liberal said, especially some years ago, that the Bible contains the Word of God and that God will make certain portions of the Bible the Word of God to the individual as he reads it. That is why neo-orthodoxy was sometimes called "crisis theology." A man is reading along and some portion of the Bible suddenly becomes the Word of God to him and this is a *crisis,* as though lightning had struck him from above. Such is the theory. But in practice each individual reader must decide for himself what is the Word of God in the Bible and what is not.

[5] J. S. Bezzant, *Objections to Christian Belief* (London: Constable and Co. Ltd., 1963), pp. 90-91.

For example, back in 1947, consider the Oslo Youth Conference which was in a period that was something of a high-water mark for neo-orthodoxy in its most hopeful form and before its problems began to show up to the neo-orthodox theologians themselves. This in a very real way was parallel to the secular existentialists' first hopefulness that was followed later on by difficulties. Think, for instance, of the early euphoria of the followers of Karl Jaspers as they accepted the concept of the final experience. As a matter of fact, there is a very specific parallel between Jaspers' term and concept of the final experience and the terms and concepts of the crisis theology. In any case, the Oslo Youth Conference officially concluded thus: "The criterion of inspiration was generally taken to be the testimony of any passage to, or its accordance with, the spirit of Jesus Christ." In other words, the young people were to decide what part of the Bible is the Word of God and what isn't on their own subjective judgment as to what part showed the spirit of Jesus Christ.

The authority which was being built in midair was and is a product of one's own subjective judgment. In short, they are saying, "Such and such is true. Why? Because I say it is true." It is at this point that Michael Green's statement that Bultmann is infallible for twenty minutes each Sunday morning is so very perceptive.

Even a cursory reading of Barth's writings and those of his followers will show that they dogmatically reject (as did the older form of liberalism) the historical view of Christianity that the original writ ings of the Bible were so inspired by God as to be kept free from error. Emil Brunner has said, "The Bible contains a lot of statements of fact, of ethics, and of doctrine, that are in contradiction to knowledge we have otherwise gained. There can be no harmony of the gospels. That is bunk, dishonesty." Brunner writes, furthermore, "This over-emphasis upon the intellectual aspect of the Faith came out in two facts—both of them well known—but, as it seems to me—never fully understood. The first of these facts was the equation of the 'Word' of the Bible with the 'Word of God'; this produced a doctrine of Verbal Inspiration, with all its disastrous results." It is interesting to note that Brunner admits that his view was not the view of Calvin, for he has written, "In the thought of Calvin a tendency to take a rigidly literal view of the Bible, which developed into the doctrine of Verbal Inspiration, comes out in the fact that Revelation and Scripture are regarded as identical." Or take the words of another representative of this position, H. T. Kerr, Jr., writing in *Theology Today,* again in the developing heyday of the hopeful era of neo-orthodoxy, "The crisis at the moment is evidenced by the transition from an older, traditional authority in terms of inerrancy and verbal infallibility to the current existential view that the Word of God is somehow written and yet apart from the words of the Bible."

It should also be pointed out that to the new liberal the Word of God comes to us through other sources than the Bible. Other religious writings, and writings that are not religious at all, can become the source of the Word of God. In this regard, Reinhold Niebuhr wrote an article in which he spoke about the place of women in the offices of the church: "Some fundamentalist theologians will seek to disinherit her by quoting texts. Perhaps the church should overcome these subChristian standards [he is not referring here to quoting texts but to the treatment of women by the church] more readily if it ceased arguing about them on Christian grounds and recognized more frankly that there are primitive depths as well as sublime heights in religion not known in secular idealism. That need not persuade us to become secularists but it might make us willing to let secular idealism speak the Word of God on occasion." In other words, to Niebuhr, there are times when secular idealism can speak the Word of God to us better than the Bible.

Incidentally, this attitude about the Bible can more recently be clearly seen in the new Roman Catholic theologians. While they say that they now give more emphasis to the Bible and less to tradition, yet their view of the Bible is now the same as Niebuhr's which has just been quoted. Therefore, they now can find parallel truths in non-Christian teachings as well.[6]

A Scandinavian Lutheran theologian has said that modern Lutheranism follows Luther in all points except his view of the Bible. Obviously, if a man does not have the Bible of Luther or Calvin, he does not have the same view of Christianity as Luther or Calvin. Calvin and Luther could speak with authority

[6] As an example, see Raymond Panikkar, *The Unknown Christ of Hinduism* (London: Darton, Longman and Todd, 1964).

and clarity because their feet were fixed on the Bible as being the Word of God; that gave them an objective and absolute standard. The new liberal cannot speak with clarity or true authority because the basis of his judgment is subjective. It is both Hegelian synthesis and Kierkegaardian upper story.

I have devoted considerable space to elucidating the nature of the new theology both in its earlier developing form and now because this is, after all, the basic form in which present-day doctrinal impurity is expressed. When the visible church faces the question of the principle of the purity of the visible church today, it finds that its primary difficulties are associated with this new theology. Hence, I feel it is important that we understand what is involved and how definitely this is related to the secular existential philosophy of today. Once again naturalistic theology is only saying the same things as naturalistic secular thought.

the new hope becomes despair

It is interesting, however, that this third step of modern upper-story mysticism with regard to the things that really matter has not produced the results that were intended. At first the new secular humanism seemed like a great hope, for even though reason leads to despair, these humanists thought meaning and hope could be found in the existential experience. But the existential experience, like all pegs hung in midair, has proved to be not a hope but a damnation.

Take, for example, the philosophy of Karl Jaspers

who, as I have said previously, says that the meaning of life must be found in the "final experience." But, of course, the final experience is completely separated from all reason and therefore one cannot talk about its content even to himself. All he can say is that he has had such an experience. It is, however, more than this. Because this type of thought has severed the meaning of life from any connection to reason, the secular or religious existentialist is left with no categories of truth, and no categories of right and wrong. Down in the lower story, reason tells him that he is only a machine, that he may be expressed with a mathematical formula. Upstairs in the upper story of non-reason, he has become something of a Greek shade unable to distinguish between fantasy and reality.

Wittgenstein in his *Tractatus* came to this same place, saying that in the area of all values, ethics, meaning and love there is nothing but silence. He then turned from his positivism and gave birth to linguistic analysis where one eventually deals only with language that leads only to language.[7]

There is evidence now that the euphoria of the new theological liberals is past and that they are also seeing the difficulties with their position just as those saying the same thing in secular terms have seen their difficulties. In other words, not only does naturalistic theology follow naturalistic humanism in its attempt at answers, but also in the despair which follows from a failure of those answers. For example, the death-of-

[7] See Chapter 3 of *He Is There and He Is Not Silent* for a more complete consideration of Wittgenstein's importance at this point.

God theology says that in the area of reason there is no reason to say that God is there. And, on the basis of naturalistic theology, that is correct. It is worth remembering here what Hedeinus said about the Lund theologians being "atheists in bishop's garments."

On the basis of liberal theology's presuppositions, every liberal theologian should be a God-is-dead theologian. But most of them still try to escape by abandoning reason and leaping into the upper story, saying that here one can have an existential, a "religious," experience. But this existential experience is completely separated from reason.

Most liberals do not like this newer (but now already very faded) God-is-dead theology, and they have objected loudly. They wish to continue to use the word *God,* but they are in the same situation as the God-is-dead theologians, because, while they use the word *God,* God is gone and every concept of a really personal God is "dead." They are left with "contentless-connotation" religious words and thus the situation still parallels the trend of secular thought.

Words like *Jesus* are separated from all reason and have no real base. So what is the word *Jesus*? A contentless banner which men take and say, in effect, "Follow me on the basis of the motivational force of the word *Jesus.*" This is really no different from modern rock groups who use the word *Jesus* in their songs. When we listen to the rock groups of 1971, what do we hear? *Jesus, Jesus, Jesus.* Don't misunderstand, most of these singers do not believe that a single word of this has anything to do with reason or with truth other than motivational "truth." Likewise in the new liberalism, seen one way, Jesus is a trip, and seen another way, he is a contentless banner that is useful in psychology and sociology.

There are some in California and elsewhere, coming out of the drug culture, who are continuing the same language and life forms and who happily are true Christians of a deep and beautiful kind. But unhappily, many of the cries of "Jesus, Jesus" heard from the Jesus freaks only equal, "Jesus is better than hash." What is the difference between these two groups? The real Christians are turning totally from the upper-story concept of the trip by turning to the clear content of the Bible.[8] They are in the stream of Bible-believing Christianity. The others still keep the upper-story trip or banner philosophy or at best they return to almost contentless emotionalism.

This is also where the modern liberal theology still is—only contentless religious words in an upper-story experience. With the non-Christian religious freaks, the word Krishna and the word Christ are interchangeable for the same reason that the modern existential theologian's ecumenism includes Hindus and Buddhists as well as any people who use the word

[8] In the light of this confusion, I would urge the true Christians (on the West Coast of the United States and other places) who are in the midst of this confusion to rapidly take the lead in making plain that they have no real relationship to the contentless groups. I certainly do not think the difference should necessarily be a difference in clothes, etc. But as true Christians it is imperative to find some way to practice truth at this point and to do so before all their advantage with those coming out of the drug culture is squandered.

Christ. In the upper story where nothing has any real content, Christ equals Krishna. It is rather like two grades of grass.

When young people say to us, "I hate God-words," if we are to be real Christians, we must say, "I hate God-words too." For such God-words are separated from all verification and falsification; they can be made to mean anything. The new theologians seem to be saying something more than secular thinkers are saying because they use such religious words. But they are really saying the same things with a different set of linguistic symbols. There is many a liberal theologian today who uses the word *God* to equal no god—to give optimism in what is to him a totally pessimistic predicament, using God-words only as a psychological tool to give psychological help or to produce sociological manipulation.

liberalism as a system
Liberalism in theology is one unified system. In a most basic sense, it did not change with the birth of existential theology. The new existential theology is no closer to the historic, biblical Christianity than is the old liberalism. It is really farther away. At least the old liberalism affirmed the concept of truth and spoke in antithesis.

Having come this far in our study of the new liberalism, it is obvious that it should be judged more completely than on some peripheral point which it produces in the area of morals or doctrine. It should not be judged, for example, because its universalism weakens evangelism but because as a total unity it is wrong. Unless we see the new liberalism as a whole and reject it as a whole, we will, to the extent that we are tolerant of it, be confused in our thinking, involved in the general intellectual irrationalism of our day and compromising in our actions.

The new theology is simply modern thought using religious words. It is under the line of anthropology, dwelling only in the world of men. It is faced with "a philosophic other" that is unknown and unknowable. The new theology is in the circle of the finite, and it has no meaning and no authority beyond the authority and the meaning which finite men can give it.

In other words, not having any propositional, verbalized communication from God to man, in all forms of liberal theology, old and new, man is on his own with only religious words rather than religious truth. Historic Christianity has nothing in common with either the old or the new secular rationalism, and it has nothing in common with either the old or the new liberal theology. Historic Christianity and either the old or the new liberal theology are two separate religions with nothing in common except certain terms which they use with totally different meanings.

adultery and apostasy: the bride and bridegroom theme*

Why should Christians and the church be concerned with doctrinal purity? This is the second of our major concerns as we investigate the principle of the practice of the purity of the visible church.

Since men today often take truth to be relative and thus look on Christian doctrine as quite unimportant, it is essential to remind ourselves that God does not look on the situation in the same way. Furthermore,

The Church at the End of the 20th Century contains two appendices, the present chapter and "The Mark of the Christian" (which has also appeared as a separate volume). Both the present book and *The Mark of the Christian* further develop the subject of *The Church at the End of the 20th Century* and thus they should be read together.

God has prevented us from doing so by very clear biblical teaching. An important part of that teaching is grounded in the statement that Christians and the church are the bride of Christ and that the bride of Christ should be kept pure and spotless before the divine bridegroom, Christ himself. In other words, the relationship between God and his people is well and properly pictured by the marriage relationship between a man and a woman. We will, therefore, investigate the Bible's view of marriage and then show how this relationship is analogous to the Christian's and the church's relationship to Jesus Christ.

the biblical norm

Ephesians 5:25b-32 reads:

> Christ also loved the church, and gave himself for it; that he might sanctify and cleanse it with the washing of water by the word, that he might present it to himself a glorious church, not having spot, or wrinkle, or any such thing; but that it should be holy and without blemish. So ought men to love their wives as their own bodies. He that loveth his wife loveth himself. For no man ever yet hated his own flesh; but nourisheth and cherisheth it, even as the Lord the church: for we are members of his body, of his flesh, and of his bones. For this cause shall a man leave his father and mother, and shall be joined unto his wife, and they two shall be one flesh. This is a great mystery: but I speak concerning Christ and the church.

Here is a remarkably strong statement about the

church as the bride of Christ. Notice, however, how God very carefully intertwines this with the normal marriage relationship. The two ideas are so fused that it is almost impossible in an exegetical study to divide them even with, as it were, an instrument as sharp as a surgeon's scalpel. Thus we have in Ephesians 5:21-25: "Submitting yourselves one to another in the fear of God. Wives, submit yourselves unto your own husbands, as unto the Lord. For the husband is the head of the wife, even as Christ is the head of the church: and he is the saviour of the body. Therefore as the church is subject unto Christ, so let the wives be to their own husbands in everything. Husbands, love your wives, even as Christ also loved the church, and gave himself for it." And verse 33: "Nevertheless let every one of you in particular so love his wife even as himself; and the wife see that she reverence her husband."

So there is here a very strong intertwining of teaching about the three relationships: the man-woman relationship, the Christ-Christian relationship and the Christ-church relationship.

In the New Testament, the brideship is thought of in two ways. Some texts emphasize the fact that each Christian is, individually, the bride of Christ, and others stress that the church as a whole is the bride of Christ. But there is no contradiction; there is merely unity in the midst of diversity. The church is collectively the bride of Christ, and it is made up of individual Christians, each one of whom is the bride of Christ.

Paul says (verse 32) that he is speaking of a great

mystery. What a tremendous mystery! The fact that Christ, the eternal second person of the Trinity, has become the divine bridegroom.

This passage in Ephesians does not stand alone. In many places in the New Testament this same sort of illustration is used intertwiningly. In John 3:28-29, we find John the Baptizer introducing Christ under these terms: "Ye yourselves bear me witness, that I said, I am not the Christ, but that I am sent before him. He [that is, the Christ] that hath the bride is the bridegroom." That is, when John introduces Christ to the Jewish people he says not only, Here is the Lamb of God, and, Here is the one who is going to be baptized by the Holy Spirit and who is going to baptize by the Holy Spirit, but also, Here is the bridegroom of the bride.

Romans 7:4 contains a very striking use of this teaching: "Wherefore, my brethren, ye also are become dead to the law by the body of Christ" (and then comes a double "in order that") "*in order that* ye should be married to another, even to him who is raised from the dead. . . ." So we are dead to the law in order that we should be married to Christ. But that is not the end of it: " . . . *in order that* we should bring forth fruit unto God." This overwhelming picture is that, as the bride puts herself in the bridegroom's arms on the wedding day and then daily, and as therefore children are born, so too the individual Christian is to put himself or herself in the bridegroom's arms, not only once for all in justification, but existentially, moment by moment, and then he will bear Christ's fruit out into the fallen, revolted, external world. In this relationship we are all female. This is the biblical picture: surely one that we would not dare use if God himself did not use it.

The Old Testament, like the New, emphasizes the bride and the bridegroom aspect. In the Old Testament it is God and his people: God is the husband of his people. In Jeremiah 3:14: "Turn, O backsliding children, saith the Lord; for I am married unto you." And, of course, there is no basic difference. The church continues. The church is new at Pentecost in one sense, yet in another sense it existed from the first man who was redeemed on the basis of Christ's coming work.

We have in 2 Corinthians 11:1-2: "Would to God ye could bear with me a little in my folly: and indeed bear with me. For I am jealous over you with godly jealousy: for I have espoused [engaged] you to one husband, that I may present you as a chaste virgin to Christ." And in the great culmination of Revelation 19:6-9 we have the picture of the church at the end of this era—when Christ has returned. What is the great event? It is nothing less than the marriage supper of the Lamb:

> And I heard as it were the voice of a great multitude, and as the voice of many waters, and as the voice of mighty thunderings, saying, Alleluia: for the Lord God omnipotent reigneth. Let us be glad and rejoice, and give honour to him: for the marriage of the Lamb is come, and his wife has made herself ready. And to her was granted that she should be arrayed in fine linen, clean and white: for the fine linen is the

righteousness of saints. And he saith unto me, Write, Blessed are they which are called unto the marriage supper of the Lamb. And he saith unto me, These are the true sayings of God.

This theme which is seen throughout the Old and New Testaments culminates in this last great Lord's Supper where Christ himself now will serve his people. And there need be no hurry and there need be no rush, with millions and millions being served from the hands of the risen Lord. And they, being risen physically from the dead, will partake with their resurrected bodies. We look forward to this as we repeat the words of 1 Corinthians 11:26 each time in the Communion service: "For as often as ye eat this bread, and drink this cup, ye do shew the Lord's death till he come."

Thus we find that the man-woman relationship of marriage is stressed throughout the Scriptures as a picture, an illustration, a type, of the wonder of the relationship of the individual and Christ and of the church and Christ. What a contrast this is to the Eastern thinking, when, for example, Shiva came out of his ice-filled cave in the Himalayas and saw a mortal woman and loved her. He put his arms around her, she disappeared and he became neuter. There is nothing like this in the Scriptures. When we accept Christ as our Savior we do not lose our personality. For all eternity our personality stands in oneness with Christ.

Just as there is a real oneness between the human bride and bridegroom who really love each other, and yet the two personalities are not confused, so in our oneness with Christ, Christ remains Christ and the bride remains the bride. This great understanding of the way Scripture parallels the human man-woman relationship and our union with Christ guides our thinking in two directions. First, it makes us understand the greatness and the wonder and the beauty of marriage and, second, it helps us to understand profoundly something of the relationship between God and his people and between Christ and his church. We understand in a real way something of this relationship as we understand in a real way something of the marriage relationship.

My personal opinion is that the marriage relationship is not just an illustration, but rather that in all things—including the marriage relationship—God's external creation speaks of himself. We properly reject pantheism, but the orthodox man is in danger of forgetting that God has created the objective world— all the parts of his external creation—not merely as an abstract apologetic, but so that it speaks of himself. While God is not the world, the world is created by God to speak about God.

the bible and sexual adultery

In our generation people are asking why promiscuous sexual relationships are wrong. I would say that there are three reasons. (There may well be more, but in this study I want to draw attention to these three.) The first one, of course, is simply because God says so. God is the creator and the judge of the universe; his character is the law of the universe, and when he tells us a thing is wrong, it *is* wrong—if we are going to have the kind of God Scripture portrays.

Second, we must never forget that God has made us in our relationships to really fulfill that which he made us to be, and therefore a right sexual relationship is for our good as we are made. It is not to our real fulfillment to have promiscuous sexual relationships. Promiscuity tries to force man into a form which God never made him for, and in which he cannot be fulfilled.

The third is the reason we are dealing with most fully in this study: Promiscuous sexual relationships are wrong because they break the picture of what God means marriage, the relationship of man and woman, to be. Marriage is set forth to be the illustration of the relationship of God and his people, and of Christ and his church. It stands upon God's character, and God is eternally faithful to his people. We who are Christians should live every day of our lives in glad recognition of the faithfulness of God to his people, a faithfulness resting upon his character and upon his covenants, his promises.

If, therefore, the relationship of God with his people rests upon his character, and if God is faithful to his people, then sexual relationship outside of marriage breaks this parallel. Thus if we break God's illustration by such a relationship, it is a serious thing. Both the Old and New Testaments speak out strongly against all sexual promiscuity—adultery and all other forms of wrong sexual relationships. Adultery means the sexual unfaithfulness of a person who is married. The Bible never allows us to tone down the utter seriousness of adultery.

In Matthew 5:32, for example, Jesus says: "But I say unto you, That whosoever shall put away his wife, saving for the cause of fornication, causeth her to commit adultery: and whosoever shall marry her that is divorced committeth adultery." In the Jewish setting engagement was tantamount to marriage, and all forms of unfaithfulness are included here. What he is saying is that unfaithfulness is so great a sin that the other person has a proper right to end the marriage upon the basis of adultery.

Then of course, in the Law in Exodus 20:14, one of the ten commandments says: "Thou shalt not commit adultery." The Old Testament was not only the religious book of the Jews, but also their book of basic civil law; as such it was related to the commands of God in the theocracy. Again, in Leviticus 20:10 God does not allow us to think that adultery is a small thing: "And the man that committeth adultery with another man's wife, even he that committeth adultery with his neighbour's wife, the adulterer and the adulteress shall surely be put to death." Furthermore Deuteronomy 22:22 reads: "If a man be found lying with a woman married to an husband [later there are other directions for the punishment of sexual intercourse with an unmarried woman], then they shall both of them die, both the man that lay with the woman, and the woman: so shalt thou put away evil from Israel."

The book of Proverbs over and over again warns against adultery and its serious consequences. In the book of Jeremiah God continues to speak concerning this. Look at the first part of verses 10 and 11 of

Jeremiah 23: "For the land is full of adulterers"; and then, "For both prophet and priest are profane." The prophet and the priest are no more free from adultery than the people. Jeremiah emphasizes the fact that indeed there is a great tragedy here: The people of God are given to adultery.

Jeremiah's prophecy came at a crucial time in the Jewish history, a time, we learn from Jeremiah 5:7-8, when the economy was affluent. But though the Jews were materially well-off, they were under the judgment of God: "How shall I pardon thee for this? thy children have forsaken me, and sworn by them that are no gods: when I had fed them to the full [here is the affluent society], they then committed adultery, and assembled themselves by troops in the harlots' houses. They were as fed horses in the morning: every one neighed after his neighbour's wife." So they are fed, they are filled with affluency, their stomachs are full of food, they have time on their hands. In this situation, what do they turn to? They are like the well-fed horse that stands and neighs on one side of the stall for the female in heat on the other side of the stall. God uses overwhelmingly strong terms in discussing adultery.

The New Testament reveals exactly the same attitude. For example, in Galatians 5:19: "Now the works of the flesh are manifest, which are these; Adultery, fornication, uncleanness, lasciviousness, idolatry, witchcraft [etc.]." This is not to say that sexual sin is worse than any other sin. Such a concept of sin is completely warped and twisted If we compare this list of sins with the other lists in the

New Testament, we will notice that sexual sin is not always, by any means, named first. The Holy Spirit very carefully breaks up the listing of the sins in the New Testament, thus indicating that, except for the great sin of turning from God, we must not put one above the other. Other sins are also sins, and so the lists sometimes mention them in one order, sometimes in another. But that is a different thing from forgetting that God very strongly condemns sexual sin. All sin is equally sin. Nevertheless, God never allows us to tone down on the condemnation of sexual sin. Sexual sin shatters the illustration of God and his people, of Christ and his church.

the bride of Christ and spiritual adultery

But there is another level in our understanding of adultery. In 2 Corinthians 11:1-2, which we have looked at before, we read: "Would to God ye could bear with me a little in my folly: and indeed bear with me. For I am jealous over you with godly jealousy: for I have espoused you to one husband, that I may present you as a chaste virgin to Christ." Here is the first step: Men have become Christians and thus are the bride of Christ. Then Paul adds this in verse 3: "But I fear, lest by any means, as the serpent beguiled Eve through his subtlety, so your minds should be corrupted from the simplicity that is in Christ." Here is the second step: The bride of Christ can be led away and can become less than the bride should be. As there can be physical adultery, so too there can be unfaithfulness to the divine bridegroom—spiritual adultery.

No one is perfect. None of us is totally faithful to our divine bridegroom. We are all weak. Many times we are unfaithful in a positive or a negative way in our thoughts or our actions. But the Scripture makes a clear distinction between the imperfection of all Christians and the spiritual adultery which results when those who claim to be God's people stop listening to what God has said and turn to other gods. As far as the Bible is concerned, the latter is apostasy.

The Bible takes the great and tremendous sin of adultery and shows us how important it is. And then it takes apostasy (turning away from God), calls it spiritual adultery (turning away from the divine bridegroom) and says, This is even more important! But isn't that to be expected? If the Bible speaks out against breaking the illustration, shattering the symbol, how much more should we expect it to condemn the violation of the reality of which marriage is the symbol!

There is a stigma in the use of the term *adultery*. Even if there has been open and blatant adultery, when a husband and wife go to the law for a divorce, they often avoid the word. A nice, gentle name is substituted. The world itself dislikes the term *adultery*. And it is the same with *apostasy*. Men like to tone down the reality and speak in polite language. But God does not. The world still winces at the term *adultery*, even in the post-Christian second half of the twentieth century; but God takes this term and applies it like a knife, crying out to his people. Over and over again *adultery* and parallel terms are used to describe God's people turning away from God.

Exodus 34:12-15 reads:

Take heed to thyself, lest thou make a covenant with the inhabitants of the land whither thou goest, lest it be for a snare in the midst of thee: but ye shall destroy their altars, break their images, and cut down their groves: for thou shalt worship no other god: for the LORD, whose name is Jealous, is a jealous God: Lest thou make a covenant with the inhabitants of the land, and they go a whoring after their gods, and do sacrifice unto their gods, and one call thee, and thou eat of his sacrifice.

When the people of God turn aside to these gods, the false gods round about, what does God call it? He says, Do you not understand what you are doing? You are going a whoring, you are caught in the midst of spiritual adultery.

Leviticus 20:5-6 also uses the strongest terms: "Then I will set my face against that man, and against his family, and will cut him off, and all that go a whoring after him, to commit whoredom with Molech [a false god I will be discussing later], from among their people." Notice here that God uses the same expression. For God's people to turn from God is spiritual adultery. Judges 2:17 says: "And yet they would not hearken unto their judges, but they went a whoring after other gods, and bowed themselves down unto them." The term "bowed themselves down unto them" is a sexual term used of a wife giving herself to her husband. And here God uses it with all this force when he says: Do you not see that you have acted like an adulterous woman bowing down in the sexual position before another man? In the book of Psalms (73:27) we read again: "For lo, they that are far from thee shall perish: thou hast destroyed all them that go a whoring from thee."

In Isaiah 1:21: "How is the faithful city become a harlot!" Who is this? This is Jerusalem, Jerusalem the golden. This is Jerusalem the city of God, Zion. What has she become? A prostitute. Why? Because she has turned from her rightful husband and become a street walker with false gods. And consider Jeremiah 3:1: "They say, If a man put away his wife, and she go from him, and become another man's, shall he return unto her again? shall not that land be greatly polluted? but thou hast played the harlot with many lovers; yet return again to me, saith the Lord." God is saying, My faithfulness, my faithfulness goes right on. What you are doing is wounding me. The New Testament says the same thing: We can make the Holy Spirit sad (Eph. 4:30). He is a person, and when we turn away from him and teach and do what is contrary to the character of God as revealed in Scripture, we wound the Holy Spirit. And the Old Testament says that when the people of God turn away from God, it is not nothing to God; it saddens the husband who is God.

Jeremiah 3:6 continues: "The Lord said also unto me in the days of Josiah the king, Hast thou seen that which backsliding Israel hath done? she is gone up upon every high mountain and under every green tree, and there hath played the harlot." Here is a picture of the hills, of the trees, of the places where they worship. And Jeremiah says, These have become your lovers. The ninth verse says: "And it came to pass through the lightness of her whoredom, that she defiled the land, and committed adultery with stones and with stocks." He says, This is what you are worshipping instead of the living God. How does God describe it? He pictures it as a perverse adultery with these objects.

In Ezekiel 6:9 God, not Ezekiel, is speaking: "I am broken with their whorish heart." God is saying about his people who have turned away into apostasy, "I am broken with their whorish heart, which has departed from me, and with their eyes, which go a whoring after their idols." Notice how God is concerned about his people. This is not a neutral thing, a matter of indifference, to God. God is not just a theological term, he is not a "philosophical other." He is a personal God and we should glory in that fact. But we must understand that since he is a personal God, he can be grieved. When his people turn away from him, there is sadness indeed on the part of the omnipotent God.

Ezekiel 16:30-32 pounds on: "How weak is thine heart, saith the Lord God, seeing thou doest all these things, the work of an imperious whorish woman; in that thou buildest thine eminent place in the head of every way [this reference is to a brothel; God is saying, Your idols built on every street corner are like a brothel] and makest thine high place in every street; and hast not been as an harlot, in that thou scornest hire; but as a wife that committeth adultery, which taketh strangers instead of her husband!" This is pursued further in Ezekiel 23, where the whole chapter is given over to this concept. God says, there are two cities, Jerusalem in the south and Samaria in the north, and they have both committed spiritual adultery, and he describes it there in the strongest terms.

Let us move on to Hosea 4:12: "My people ask counsel at their stocks, and their staff declareth unto them: for the spirit of whoredoms hath caused them to err, and they have gone a whoring from under their God." Notice the last expression again, where the sexual picture is used so vividly. God says, This is what you have done, you have moved out and you have taken this position under another god, a god that is no god—a god that is nonsense, nothing more than a stick, nothing more than your own staff. You commit spiritual adultery with these things; this is who you are and what you are and where you are.

Notice also Hosea 4:13: "They sacrifice upon the tops of the mountains, and burn incense upon the hills, under oaks and poplars and elms, because the shadow thereof is good: therefore your daughters shall commit whoredom, and your spouses shall commit adultery." This points to another whole stream of biblical teaching that I will not discuss here except in connection with this one verse: The Old Testament says that if God's people turn away in spiritual adultery, it will not be long until the following generations are engaged in physical adultery, for the two things go hand in hand. And if any generation proves this, it is our generation. John Updike is right in his book *The Couples.* The whole novel is an illustration of the last pages: Here the church is burned down. In reality the church was "burned down" before the book began, and there was nothing left for Piet, the main character, except his promiscuous sexual life.

Our generation proves this with overflowing force. Let there be spiritual adultery and it will not be long until physical adultery sprouts like toadstools in the land. In the 1930s liberalism took over almost all the churches in the United States and in the 1960s our generation is sick with promiscuous sex. It is the same in Britain and other countries. These things are not unrelated: They are cause and effect.

Again in Hosea 9:1 we read: "Rejoice not, O Israel, for joy, as other people: for thou hast gone a whoring from thy God, thou hast loved a reward upon every cornfloor." Here again in Hosea 9 apostasy is spiritual adultery. Notice the form of speech God uses. A woman is out harvesting, and there is a freedom in the midst of the harvest. She takes a gift of money from some man to sleep with him on the cornfloor in the midst of the harvesting. This is what those who had been God's people had become: The wife of the living God is this in her apostasy.

You may say now, have we not read enough of these verses? We have not read the half of what we will find as we go through the Scriptures. God says, I do not want you to forget, I do not look upon spiritual adultery lightly.

I have deliberately chosen examples from all parts of the Old Testament—sections from the law, from different places in the historical books, from the books of poetry and from the prophets. The whole of the Old Testament speaks in the same terms and carries the same force, the same thrust.

You may say, is this not just an Old Testament view? The answer is, No, it is the way the New Testament speaks as well. Revelation 17:1-5 reads:

And there came one of the seven angels which had the seven vials, and talked with me, saying unto me, Come hither; I will shew unto thee the judgment of the great whore that sitteth upon many waters: with whom the kings of the earth have committed fornication, and the inhabitants of the earth have been made drunk with the wine of her fornication. So he carried me away in the spirit into the wilderness: and I saw a woman sit upon a scarlet coloured beast, full of names of blasphemy, having seven heads and ten horns. And the woman was arrayed in purple and scarlet colour, and decked with gold and precious stones and pearls, having a golden cup in her hand full of abominations and filthiness of her fornication: And upon her forehead was a name written, MYSTERY, BABYLON THE GREAT, THE MOTHER OF HARLOTS AND ABOMINATIONS OF THE EARTH.

The Bible just slams the door. This language is definitely not in the Old Testament alone. It is brought to its highest pitch in the New Testament when the apostate church of the last days, and the culture it produces, is described in these terms.

spiritual adultery today

Now, let us notice where we have come. When those

who claim to be God's people turn aside from the Word of God and from the Christ of history, this is more heinous in the sight of God than the worst case of infidelity in marriage, for it destroys the reality, the great central bridegroom-bride relationship. I have taken care to emphasize that God does not minimize promiscuity in sexual relationships, but apostasy—spiritual adultery—is worse. And the modern liberal theologian is in that place. How do we look at it? I would suggest we must be careful to look at it no less clearly than God does. Consider the liberal theology of our day. It denies the personal *God who is there.* It denies the divine historic Christ. It denies the Bible as God's verbalized Word. It denies God's way of salvation. The liberals elevate their own humanistic theories to a position above the Word of God, the revealed communication of God to men. They make gods which are no gods, but are merely the projection of their own minds.

As we describe their theories, we tend to dress them up in polite terms, in fine clothes, carefully weaving these clothes so as not to offend. We dress up our attitudes and statements in fine words in regard to the modern Roman Catholic Church, and we call it "the progressive theology." But it is not the progressive theology, it is a regressive theology, a humanism being spoken in classical Roman Catholic terms. In Protestantism, we call it "liberalism," which is a strange word to apply to it, for it is only humanism spoken in classical Protestant terms.

Of course, we must treat men as human beings while having discourse with them, and that very much includes the liberal theologians. We must treat them as made in the image of God, even if they are actively in rebellion against God, and we must let them know that we love them as individuals. But this does not mean that we should forget that apostasy must be named as apostasy. Apostasy must be called what it is—a spiritual adultery. We must have politeness, and struggle for human relationships with the liberal theologians with whom we discuss. But as to the system they teach, there is to be no toning down concerning what it is—spiritual adultery. As I said, in our generation we tend to tone down the word *adultery* in divorce cases, for we do not much like the word. Far more in the religious realm do we tone down the terms *spiritual adultery* and *apostasy*. But in doing this we are grievously wrong, because the Bible's perspective should be our own, and this is the way God speaks of it and looks upon it, and so this is the way God's people are called to look upon it.

This spiritual adultery is worse, much worse, than physical adultery. But it is also much worse, let me say, than the Jews following their idols. Oh, how God spoke out against the Jews following their idols! What strong figures of speech he used in love in order to bring them to their senses! But modern liberal theology is far worse, for it turns against greater light, against greater blessing. Modern liberal theology is worse than following the Molech of old.

Molech, whose idol was in the valley of Hinnon, was a heathen god whom the Jews were constantly warned against following. And what a god he was! The central act of his worship was the sacrifice of the first-born of every woman's body. According to one tradition, there was an opening at the back of the brazen idol, and after a fire was made within it, each parent had to come and with his own hands place his first-born child in the white-hot, outstretched hands of Molech. According to this tradition the parent was not allowed to show emotion, and drums were beaten so that the baby's cries could not be heard as it died in the hands of Molech.

There, I would say, stand many in our day. Many of those who come to me, those with whom I work, are the children destroyed by a worse than Molech. Men—men who were supposedly the men of God— have stood by while the children were eaten up by modern theology. And then we are told to show no emotion.

Some of us bear marks of these things from the background from which we come. All of us are marked in some way because our Western post-Christian world has been undercut by liberal theology. Every scar this present generation has, every tear cried, every baby which some of you who read this have willfully aborted, every drug trip you have taken, cannot be separated from the fact that the church has turned away and become unfaithful. Men of this generation are babies in the hands of Molech. And are we, as mere dilettantes, supposed to stand by, hear their cries and cover them up by beating loudly the drums of a profitless discussion? I tell you, No. We are to weep and to act.

What is the liberal theology like? It can only be paralleled with what God says in Proverbs 30:20

about the adulterous woman: "Such is the way of an adulterous woman; she eateth, and wipeth her mouth, and saith, I have done no wickedness." What a picture! Not everyone whose theology has been somewhat infiltrated by liberal theology should be likened to this, but the real liberal theologian (whether the old liberal or the newer existential theologian) stands in this place. They say they have done no evil by their spiritual adultery, while not only the church but the whole post-Christian culture shows the results of their unfaithfulness.

There is no adulterous woman who has ever been so soiled as the liberal theology, for it has had all the gifts of God and has turned away to worship something more destructive than Molech was to the babies of their idolatrous parents. This is not a thing to take lightly. We must show love to the man with whom we discuss. We must fight for the fact that he is not to be treated as less than a man. Nothing is more ugly than the orthodox man treating another man as less than a man, failing to show that he takes seriously Christ's teaching that all men are our neighbors. We do not discuss with the liberal only to win, but to help others, and to try to help him as well. But to treat lightly what liberal theology has done—not for a moment!

God's word for our generation
What does God say to our generation? Exactly the same thing that he said to Israel two thousand five hundred years ago when he said through Ezekiel: "I am broken with their whorish heart, which hath

departed from me, and with their eyes, which go a whoring after their idols." I believe that this is how God looks at much of the modern church and at our Western culture. I believe that this is how he looks at much of our cinema, much of our drama, much of our art. And above everything else this is the way he looks at the churches in which a gospel that is no gospel is being preached. God is saddened. Should *we* not be moved?

He is the same God, he is the living God, he is the unchanging God. He is the God who is there. And will he not do in the midst of this situation what he did in the midst of the Jewish situation in the time of Isaiah in the Northern Kingdom, and in the time of Jeremiah and Ezekiel and Daniel in the Southern Kingdom? Will he not judge our culture? Will he not call it adulterous? I tell you in the name of God he will judge our culture, and he *is* judging our culture.

Now, what should be our response? Listen to Jeremiah speak in 13:27: "Woe unto thee, O Jerusalem! Woe unto thee, O Jerusalem!" Indeed, as redeemed men we should know the joy of Christ, but as we look around us at much of the church and at much of our culture, can we fail to weep? Must we not also have this message? "Woe unto thee, O Jerusalem! Woe unto thee, O Jerusalem!" For like Jerusalem, much of the church has turned apostate. Within two or three generations in our Northern European countries we have turned aside. In Germany over a longer period, but in most of our countries so quickly have we turned aside: "Woe unto you, Woe unto you, O Jerusalem! Woe to you, O liberal church! Woe to you, O apostate Christendom!" We must say these words while we cry for the individual and while we never fail to treat him as a human being. We must not speak more lightly than Jeremiah. We must not be any less moved. Our response must not be merely a theoretical discussion of an intellectual nature. It must be the cry, "Woe, O liberal church! Woe, O apostate Christendom!"

It is not just a question of abstract theology that is involved, not just an academic difference. It is not that I should get my Ph.D. and go off and sit in some faculty and merely make polite academic conversation. It is the difference between loyalty to the living God and spiritual adultery—spiritual adultery against the Creator and the Judge of the universe. Spiritual adultery, mind you, against the only adequate bridegroom for Man—individual man and mankind—the only adequate bridegroom for all men in all the world. Spiritual adultery against the only one who can fulfill the longing of the human heart. To turn away from the divine bridegroom is to turn to unfulfilledness. This is not only sin: It is destruction.

We have seen how desperately wrong and sinful physical adultery is, but notice that Jesus gives a priority. In Matthew 21:31 Jesus says to the religious leaders of his day: "Verily I say unto you, That the publicans and the harlots go into the kingdom of God before you." It is not that Jesus minimized the sexual sin, but here he tells the religious leaders of his day who have turned away from God that the harlots and those who collect taxes for the Romans will go into the kingdom of God before them. As these men walk through the streets and see such a woman, they will not speak to her. They will not even look at her. They turn away from her. They show their disgust publicly. But Jesus is saying, Look at her! Don't you understand? She will get into the kingdom of God before you ever will. Both are sinful. But God himself in the words of Christ puts down a priority. Sexual sin is sinful, but spiritual adultery is overwhelmingly worse.

What is apostasy? It is spiritual adultery. No other words will do. This must be taken into account as we speak of the practice of the purity of the visible church. Do not be only academic when you speak concerning the new Molech. You yourself have the burn marks of the new Molech. Nobody escapes, even if he has been raised in a Christian home and has been a Christian from the time he was young. There is not one of us in our culture who does not have some burn marks from the new Molech upon his skin—not one.

God's word for us

But for ourselves, we who by God's grace belong to the people of God, we who are Christ's, we who are God's, we who have been redeemed on the basis of the blood of the Lamb—let us understand that we are now called, on the basis of this study, to take one more most crucial step. We are *to act* as that which we are. Who are we? We are not just those going to heaven: We are even now the wife of God. We are at this moment the bride of Christ. And what does our divine bridegroom want from us? He wants not only doctrinal faithfulness, but our love day by day.

I must ask myself, "What about you, Schaeffer?" And what about you, each one of you who know the grace of God? What should be your attitude? Our attention must swing back now to ourselves.

We must ask, Do I fight merely for doctrinal faithfulness? This is like the wife who never sleeps with anybody else but never shows love to her own husband. Is that a sufficient relationship in marriage? No, ten thousand times no. Yet if I am a Christian who speaks and acts for doctrinal faithfulness but do not show love to my divine bridegroom, I am in the same place as such a wife. What God wants from us is not only doctrinal faithfulness, but our love day by day. Not in theory, mind you, but in practice.

Those of us who are children of God must realize the seriousness of modern apostasy; we must urge each other not to have any part in it. But at the same time we must be the loving, true bride of the divine bridegroom in reality and in practice, day by day, in the midst of the spiritual adultery of our day. Our call is first to be the bride faithful, but that is not the total call. The call is not only to be the bride faithful, but also to be the bride in love.

practicing purity in the visible church

Born-again Christians, whatever their background—Reformed, Lutheran, Baptist, Brethren, Congregational, Anglican or whatever their distinctives—have certain basic things in common. One of these is this task: to exhibit simultaneously the holiness of God and the love of God.

In *The Mark of the Christian* I have expressed and developed this thought in a slightly different way. There I have written about the need *simultaneously* to practice two biblical principles. The first is the principle of the practice of the purity of the visible church (not the invisible church we join when by God's grace we cast ourselves upon Christ, but the visible church). The Scriptures teach that we must *practice,* not just *talk* about, the purity of the visible church. The second is the principle of an observable love and oneness among all *true* (note the emphasis) Christians. *The Mark of the Christian* stresses from John 13:34-35 that, according to Jesus himself, the world has the right to decide whether we are true Christians, true disciples of Christ, on the basis of the love we show to all true Christians. John 17:21 provides something even more sobering in that here Jesus gives the world the right to judge whether the Father has sent the Son on the basis of whether the world sees observable love among all true Christians.

In *The Church at the End of the 20th Century,* I emphasize another related parallelism: the call of God to simultaneously practice the orthodoxy of doctrine and the orthodoxy of community in the visible church. The latter of these we have too often all but forgotten. But one cannot explain the explosive dynamite, the *dunamis,* of the early church apart from the fact that they practiced two things simultaneously: orthodoxy of doctrine and orthodoxy of community in the midst of the visible church, a community which the world could see. By the grace of God, therefore, the church must be known simultaneously for its purity of doctrine and the reality of its community. Our churches have so often been only preaching points with very little emphasis on community, but exhibition of the love of God in practice is beautiful and must be there.

We have, then, two sets of parallel couplets: (1) the principle of the practice of the purity of the visible church and yet the practice of observable love among all true Christians; and (2) the practice of orthodoxy of doctrine and observable orthodoxy of community in the visible church.

The heart of these sets of principles is to show forth the love of God and the holiness of God *simultaneously.* If we show either of these without the other, we exhibit not the character, but a caricature of God for the world to see. If we stress the love of God without the holiness of God, it turns out only to be compromise. But if we stress the holiness of God without the love of God, we practice something that is hard and lacks beauty. And it is important to show forth beauty before a lost world and a lost generation. All too often young people have not been wrong in saying that the church is ugly. In the name of our Lord Jesus Christ we are called upon to show to a watching world and to our own young people that the church is something beautiful.

Several years ago I wrestled with the question of what was wrong with much of the church that stood for purity. I came to the conclusion that in the flesh we can stress purity without love or we can stress the love of God without purity, but that in the flesh we cannot stress both simultaneously. In order to exhibit both simultaneously, we must look moment by moment to the work of Christ, to the work of the Holy Spirit. Spirituality begins to have real meaning in our moment-by-moment lives as we begin to exhibit simultaneously the holiness of God and the love of God.

Let us consider, then, the exhibition of the

holiness of God in relationship to the purity of the visible church. To do this, I want to go back into history. I will use the United States, first, because it is my own country and, second, because in the United States the whole course of events has occurred in a much shorter period than in most other countries and therefore can be seen and comprehended easily, though most countries have gone or are going through parallel situations. I come from the Presbyterian tradition. I will go back into the Presbyterian history of the 1930s and beg those of other backgrounds to learn from our mistakes.

In the 1930s almost every large denomination in the United States came under the control of liberalism. The Presbyterian Church in the U.S.A. (now called the United Presbyterian Church) is one of the clearest cases of all because it was a very strong doctrinal church, and thus the shift can be clearly observed. I do not mean that everyone in the Presbyterian Church (or in these other denominations) became liberal; certainly not every pastor became liberal, but the denomination as a denomination came definitely under the control of those who held to liberal theology.

Let us go back first of all to 1924, one year after the Auburn Affirmation was signed. In the Presbyterian Church the Auburn Affirmation was the liberals' public declaration of war upon the historic Christian faith. It threw down the gauntlet. The conservatives of the church decided that the way to meet this challenge was to elect a moderator of the General Assembly who would clearly be Bible-believing. As a result, 1924 saw elected as the moderator of the Northern Presbyterian Church an orthodox, Bible-believing man, Dr. Clarence Edward McCartney. The conservatives were jubilant. The secular newspapers carried the story of the conservative victory, and the conservatives rejoiced. But while all the rejoicing was going on, the liberals consolidated their power in the church bureaucracy. And because they were allowed to do so, the election of the conservative moderator proved to mean nothing. By 1936 the liberals were so in control that they were able to defrock Dr. J. Gresham Machen, putting him out of the ministry.[1]

It seems to me that by the end of the 1930s all but three of the major Protestant denominations in the United States came under the control of those

---

[1] Machen's defrocking and the resulting division of the Northern Presbyterian Church was front-page news in the secular news media in much of the country. However much conscious foresight this showed on the editors' and broadcasters' part, this was rightfully page-one news, for it marked the culmination of the drift of the Protestant churches from 1900 to 1936. It was this drift that laid the base for the cultural, sociological, moral, legal and governmental changes from that time to the present. Without this drift in the churches, I am convinced that the changes from a rural to urban society, etc., would not have produced the same results they now have. When the Reformation churches shifted, the Reformation consensus was undercut. A good case could be made out that the news about Machen was the most significant U.S. news in the first half of the 20th century. It was the culmination of a long trend toward liberalism within the Presbyterian Church and represented the same trend in most other denominations. Even if we were interested only in sociology, this change in the churches and the resulting shift to a post-Christian sociological base is important to understand if we are to grasp what is happening in the United States and other Northern European Reformation countries today.

holding liberal theological views, and that now in the 1970s all three of these are in the same place of decision as the other denominations were in the 1930s. It is to be noted that the control of the Roman Catholic Church is now also firmly in the hands of the progressives led by existential theologians who believe and teach the same things as the existential theologians in the Protestant churches do but using traditional Roman Catholic, rather than Protestant, terms.

Two of the three Protestant denominations in the United States now in the place of decision, interestingly enough, have at this time tried to protect themselves, as did the Northern Presbyterian Church, by electing a conservative executive officer. But I would urge the true Christians today in these denominations to learn from the mistakes of the Presbyterian Church: Do not think that merely because a Bible-believing man is elected as an executive officer or is appointed to an important position, that this will give safety to a denomination. There must be an exhibition of the *practice* of the purity of the visible church in any denomination if it is really to dwell in safety. The holiness of God must be exhibited in ecclesiastical affairs. We must practice truth, not just speak about it.

It must be understood that the new humanism and the new theology have no concept of true truth. Hegelian relativism has triumphed in the church as well as in the university and in society. The true Christian, however, is called upon not only to teach truth but to practice truth in the midst of such relativism. And if we are ever to practice truth, it certainly must be in a day such as ours.

This means, among other things, that, after we have done all we can on a personal level, if they persist in their liberalism, the liberals in the church should come under discipline. For, as I pointed out in the preceding chapter, the church must remain the faithful bride of Christ. And, as I explained in detail in the first chapter, the liberals are not faithful to the God of the Bible, the God who is there. Historic Christianity, biblical Christianity, believes that Christianity is not just doctrinal truth, but flaming truth, true to what is there, true to the great final environment, the infinite-personal God. Liberalism, on the other hand, is unfaithfulness, spiritual adultery toward the divine bridegroom. We are involved, therefore, in a matter of loyalty, loyalty not only to the creeds, but to the Scripture and beyond that to the divine bridegroom—the infinite-personal divine bridegroom who is there in an absolute antithesis to his not being there.

We not only believe in the existence of truth, but we believe we have the truth—a truth that has content and can be verbalized (and *then* can be lived)—a truth we can share with the 20th-century world. Do you think our contemporaries will take us seriously if we do not practice truth? Do you think for a moment that the really tough-minded 20th-century youngsters—our own youth as they go off to universities, as they are taught in the fields of sociology, psychology, philosophy, etc., that all is relative—will take us seriously? In an age that does not believe that truth exists, do you really believe they will take seriously that their fathers are speaking truth and believe in truth? Will their fathers have credibility, if they do not practice truth and do not practice antithesis in religious matters?

It is therefore necessary for the true Christians in the church to oppose McLuhanesque "cool" communication employed by the liberal theologians with the "hot" communication of theological and biblical content.[2] It is only thus that we can practice the exhibition of the holiness of God.

---

[2] According to Marshall McLuhan in his theory of communication, *hot* communication is communication that has content, that appeals to men and moves men through the mind on the basis of that content. *Cool* communication is a kind of personal first-order experience wherein one is moved but without any content passing through his mind, his reason. It is a manipulation based on electronics. Father John Culkin, Director of the Communications at Fordham University, a follower of McLuhan, says this: "Gutenberg came and the Reformation came. Electronics comes and the ecumenical movement comes." He means that the ecumenical movement is rooted for its unity in the midst of a contentless situation, a situation that is completely cool and has nothing to do with objective doctrinal truth. I feel he is right. I do not believe that the modern ecumenical movement could have been built even in the day of the old liberals. The ecumenical movement is built, I believe, in organizational oneness on the basis of a lack of content.

Equally, the new existential theologians in our churches live only in the area of cool communication. They have denied content—content is not important to them. An existential, upper-story experience is separated from all reason and from all that is open either to verification or falsification. T. H. Huxley in 1890 saw that the day would come when theology would be separated from everything that has anything to do with fact and as such would never be open to challenge (*Science and Hebrew Tradition,* Vol. 4 of *Collected Essays* [Macmillan, London, 1902]) but, of course, that kind of theology doesn't mean anything either. If a thing has no point for possible verification or falsification, it is without meaning; it is only a "religious truth" in an upper-story situation.

We believe in the hot communication of content, and as our age cools off more and more in its communication, as content is played down and reason is plowed under, I believe the historic Christian faith must more and more emphasize content, content, content and then more content. In this we are brought face to face in a complete antithesis with the existential theologian. If we are to talk truth at all, we must have content on the basis of antithesis and to do this we must have discipline with regard to those who depart from the historic Christian faith. It is thus that we can practice the exhibition of the holiness of God.

At the same time, however, we must show forth the love of God to those with whom we differ. Thirty-five years ago in the Presbyterian crisis in the United States, we forgot that. We did not speak with love about those with whom we differed, and we have been paying a high price for it ever since. We must love men, including the existential theologians, even if they speak only with cool communication and have given up content entirely. We must deal with them as our neighbors, for Christ gave us the second commandment telling us that we are to love all men as our neighbors.

We must stand clearly for the principle of the purity of the visible church, and we must call for the appropriate discipline of those who take a position which is not according to Scripture. But at the same time we must visibly love them as people as we speak and write about them. We must show it before both the church and the world. We must say that the liberals are desperately wrong and that they require discipline in and by the church, but we must do so in terms that show it is not merely the flesh speaking. This is beyond us, but not beyond the work of the Holy Spirit. I regret that years ago we did not do this in the Presbyterian Church; we did not talk of the need to show love as we stood against liberalism, and, as the Presbyterian Church was lost, that lack has cost us dearly.

But with prayer both love and concern for truth can be shown. Several years ago at the Roosevelt University auditorium in Chicago, I had a dialogue with James Pike. I asked those in L'Abri to pray for one thing—that I would be able to present a clear Christian position to him and to the audience and at the same time end with a good human relationship between the two of us. It was something I could not do in myself, but God answered that prayer. A clear statement was raised, with a clear statement of differences, without destroying him as a human being. At the close he said, "If you ever come to California, please visit me in Santa Barbara." Later, when Edith and I were out in Santa Barbara, we went to his place and were able to carry on further a discussion with him without one iota of compromise, and yet again not destroying him but letting him know that we respected him as a human being.

We also talked about the possibility that his belief that he was talking to his son "on the other side" was really a matter of demonology. And James Pike did not get angry, though he was close to crying. It is possible to make clear statements, even the necessary negative ones, if simultaneously we treat men as men.

I will never forget the last time I saw him as Edith and I were leaving the Center for the Study of Democratic Institutions. He said one of the saddest things I have ever heard: "When I turned from being agnostic, I went to Union Theological Seminary, but when I graduated all that it left me was a handful of pebbles."

Who is responsible for the tragedy of James Pike? His liberal theological professors who robbed him of everything real and human. We cannot take lightly the fact that liberal theological professors in any theological school are leaving young men with a handful of pebbles and nothing more.

Yet, even in the midst of this situation, by God's grace we must do two things simultaneously: We must do all that is necessary for the purity of the visible church to exhibit the holiness of God, and yet, no matter how bitter the liberals become or what nasty things they say or what they release to the press, we must show forth the love of God in the midst of the strongest speaking we can do. If we let down one side or the other, we will not bear our testimony to God who is holy and who is love.

Let us again go back to the Presbyterian struggles of the 30s when true Christians did not remember to keep this balance. On the one hand, they waited far too long to exert discipline, and so they lost the denomination, as did the Christians in almost every other denomination. On the other hand, some of them treated the liberals as less than human, and therefore they learned such bad habits that, later, when those who formed new groups developed minor differences among themselves, they continued to treat each other badly. Beware of the habits you learn in controversy. Both must appear together: the holiness of God and the love of God exhibited simultaneously by the grace of God. It will not come automatically. It takes prayer. You must write about it in your denominational papers. You must talk about it to your congregations, you must preach sermons pointing out the necessity of standing for the holiness of God and the love of God *simultaneously,* and by your attitude you must exhibit it to your congregations and to your own children.

It is important to notice the principle we are speaking about here and the language we use to express that principle. It is not the principle of *separation.* It is *the practice of the principle of the purity of the visible church.* Words are important at this point, because we make attitudes with the words we choose and use year after year. So I repeat: The principle is the practice of the purity of the visible church. That principle may have to be exhibited in various ways, but that is the principle. The church belongs to those who by the grace of God are faithful to the Scriptures. Almost every church has in its history a process for exercising discipline, and when needed this should be used in the practice of the positive principle.

Dr. Briggs was put out of the ministry of the Presbyterian Church in the late 1890s because he was the first man who brought liberalism into Union Theological Seminary. But by the 1930s the older type liberals were able to put out Dr. Machen because of his clear stand for the Scriptures and for the gospel.

Think: Before 1900 Dr. Briggs could be disciplined; in the 1930s Dr. Machen was disciplined and put out of the ministry. What had happened in the intervening years? Discipline had not been consistently applied by the faithful men of the church. The church was able, indeed, to discipline Dr. Briggs, but after that faithful men waited too long. Though they had achieved one outstanding victory, after that first burst of discipline, they did nothing until it was far too late. Discipline in the church as in the family is not something that can be done in one great burst of enthusiasm, one great conference, one great anything. Men must be treated in love as human beings, but it is a case of continual, moment-by-moment, existential care, for we are not dealing with a merely human organization but with the church of Christ. Hence, the practice of the purity of the visible church first means discipline to those who do not take a proper position in regard to the teaching of Scripture and to the creeds.

Why is it so unthinkable today to have discipline? Why is it that at least two denominations in the United States are now so much in the hands of the liberals that it is officially and formally no longer possible to have a discipline trial, ever—even in theory? It is because both the world and the liberal church have become Hegelian and totally caught up with synthesis and relativism. It was not unthinkable to our forefathers to conduct discipline hearings because they believed that truth existed. But because the world and the liberal church no longer believe in truth as truth, any concept of discipline in regard to doctrine has become unthinkable.

I believe that all three of the larger Protestant denominations which were not lost in the 30s are today in the midst of this battle of which we are speaking. To make the ecclesiastical sweep complete, we must note that since Vatican II the Roman Catholic Church has been taken over by the progressive theologians—existential theologians using Roman Catholic terms. Thus the view of existential theologians now controls most of the ecclesiastical field.

When a church (like the Northern Presbyterian Church thirty-five years ago) comes to the place where it can no longer exert discipline, then with tears before the Lord we must consider a second step. If the battle for doctrinal purity is lost, we must understand that there is a second step to take in regard to the practice of the principle of purity of the visible church. It may be necessary for true Christians to leave the visible organization with which they have been associated. But note well: If we must leave our church, it should always be with tears—not with drums playing and flags flying. This is no place for naturally bombastic men to bombast.

We are not practicing separation. Separation is a negative concept and builds a poor mentality. The Bible's final emphasis is never on negation but on affirmation. The Bible's principle of the practice of purity of the visible church is a positive concept.

Still, we must decide what price we are willing to

pay for maintaining this principle. If we do not, then we are not free under Christ. I recall a bright young girl who was teaching at a British university. She and her husband are committed Christians, brilliant; both of them have taught in British universities. At one time she was teaching social science in a university where a behaviorist was the head of the department. He insisted that she either teach her social science on the basis of behaviorism or leave. It was a big decision for her, but fortunately she and her husband had previously prayed about it and had already agreed that in such a situation Christ was first and their academic position was secondary. Is there any other possibility for a Christian who really loves Christ?

If sacrifice is necessary in the case of a young professor, it is certainly the case in ecclesiology. And if the decision concerning cost must be faced ahead of time by Christians in academic situations, then the same decision must be faced by the institutional church. Before we ever come to a place where this horrible decision in regard to a church must be made, a prior issue must be already settled. The church as an organization is not first; Christ is first. Therefore, once Christ is no longer King and Lord in a church, then that church cannot have our loyalty. If we ever have to come to this second stage of the practice of the principle of the purity of the visible church, I pray that Christ will be put first in our decision.

If, unhappily, the Christians of a church come to this place, then I would suggest that there is another lesson to be learned from what I have observed as I have worked with various churches over many countries. We must face the fact that if we come to that unhappy moment it will not be a simple situation where all the faithful Christians will come out at the same time. And this sets up an emotional tension among *true* Christians. I watched it in the Presbyterian Church as a young man. I have watched it in other countries—for example, in Holland and England. Those who have stood side by side for years —suddenly there is a tension between them.

This results in two different tendencies. First, those who come out tend to become hard; they tend to become absolutists even in the lesser points of doctrine. One must realize that there is a great difference between believing in absolutes and having an absolutist mentality about everything. They tend to lose their Christian love for those *true* Christians who do not come out. Men who have been friends for years suddenly become estranged.

Second, those who stay in have an opposite tendency toward a growing latitudinarianism; this has tended to happen in evangelical circles in the United States. The tendency is to go from ecclesiastical latitudinarianism to cooperative comprehensiveness. Thus Christians may still talk about truth but tend less and less to practice truth. The next step comes very quickly, say, in two generations. If one stays in a denomination that is completely dominated by liberals and he gives in to the ecclesiastical latitudinarianism which becomes a cooperative comprehensiveness, there is a tendency to drift into doctrinal comprehensiveness and especially to let down on a clear view of Scripture.

There is, therefore, a danger for both those who come out and those who stay in. And in the name of the Lord Jesus Christ we must face these dangers in order to help each other. If a division comes, true Christians must not polarize. In the Presbyterian Church in 1936 we made this mistake, and we have never fully recovered from it. Most of those who left totally broke off fellowship with true brothers in Christ who stayed in.

In 1936, when Dr. Machen was going to be put out of the church, the General Assembly was meeting in Syracuse, New York. The leading conservative Presbyterian pastor in Syracuse, the Rev. Walter Watson of the First Ward Presbyterian Church, did something which showed great ecclesiastical courage. The Sunday before the General Assembly acted, he opened his pulpit to Dr. Machen. Dr. Machen preached with everyone knowing that before the next Sunday he was going to be defrocked by a liberally controlled General Assembly.

The following week *The Philadelphia Bulletin* (June 11, 1936) carried an article with a heading, "New Church Gets under Way: Presbyterian Constitutional Covenant Union Dissolves." Just a headline, but what did it mean? *The Philadelphia Bulletin* reported that the Rev. Walter Watson who had shown such courage the week before had said to those who were leaving the church: You must start a new church, but I plead with you in the name of the Lord Jesus Christ not to dissolve the Constitutional Covenant Union. This Constitutional Covenant Union was the organization to which the Bible-believing Christians within the Presbyterian Church belonged. The newspaper article read as follows:

The Rev. Watson asked for less haste in dissolving the Union. He pointed out that there were thousands in the established church "who had not seen the light yet and the only way we can reach them is through an organization similar to the Covenant Union." "I foresee," he said, "that for a while at least this new denomination will only be a little one with only a dozen churches, but in five or ten years we can expect several hundred thousand members."

Instead of following his advice, those who came out dissolved the Union and largely ceased to have any fellowship with the true brothers in Christ who had stood with them in the battle up to that moment. For thirty-five years we have painfully suffered for this decision.

Here is what happened. Since they largely broke off fellowship with the true Christians in the established church and had little or nothing to do with them, the Reformed churches in this country—both in the North and the South—have become more and more liberal. The true Christians who remained in those churches became discouraged by the attitude of those who had already left, and so they remained in the established churches. Man after man has talked to me in the last four or five years saying, "Back there I was hurt, I was injured. And because of that I have just stayed where I am, and I have been discouraged." Surely both they and those who came out but who forgot the mark of the Christian must bear the responsibility for this. And let us realize that the situation is not uniquely American. I have seen the same unhappy thing in European countries during the twenty-four years that I have lived and worked here.

Thus, it is clear, we discourage our brothers in Christ unless consciously and prayerfully ahead of time we are prepared for the situation—ready with a simultaneous, clear doctrinal stand and an exhibition of real, *observable* love among true Christians. This must be consciously thought about and prayed about and written about, for it does not come automatically. In the moment itself, tensions run high and there is little time for working on our attitudes then.

I plead with you, therefore, if, or when, that moment comes for you, that you find some way to show an observable love among *true* Christians before the world. Don't divide into ugly parties. If you do, the world will see an ugliness which will turn it off. Your children will see the ugliness, and you will lose some of your sons and daughters. They will hear such harsh things from your lips against men that they know have been your friends that they will turn away from you. Don't throw your children away, don't throw other people away by forgetting to observe, by God's grace, the two principles simultaneously—to show love and to practice the purity of the visible church.

Finally, we must not forget that the world is on fire. We are not only losing the church, but our entire culture as well. We live in the post-Christian world which is under the judgment of God. I believe today that we must speak as Jeremiah. Some people think that just because the United States of America is the United States of America, because Britain is Britain, they will not come under the judgment of God. This is not so. I believe that we of Northern Europe since the Reformation have had such light as few others have ever possessed. We have walked upon that light in our culture. Our cinemas, our novels, our art museums scream out as they walk upon that light. And worst of all, modern theology screams out as it walks upon that light. Do you think God will not judge our countries simply because they are our countries? Do you think that the holy God will not judge?

And if this is so in our moment of history, we need each other. Let us keep our doctrinal distinctives. Let us talk to each other about our distinctives as we keep our distinctives.

But in a day like ours let us recognize the proper hierarchy of things. The real chasm is not between the Presbyterians and everybody else, or the Lutherans and everybody else, or the Anglicans and everybody else, or the Baptists and everybody else, etc. The real chasm is between those who have bowed to the living God and thus also to the verbal, propositional communication of God's Word, the Scriptures, and those who have not.

As a Bible-believing Presbyterian I feel very close to true Christians from other traditions and true Christians with other distinctives. I feel no separation in Christ. I come and I shake their hands and I speak as though I have known them forever. If we get down to certain points of doctrine, we differ, but the things that I have spoken of here are not rooted in Presbyterianism or in other distinctives, they are rooted in historic Christianity and in the Scriptural faith. While I feel close to Bible-believing Christians who are not Presbyterians, I am not close to non-Bible-believing Presbyterians. This is where the division lies.

So in a day like ours, when the world is on fire, let us be careful to keep things in proper order. Let us find ways to show the world that while we maintain and do not minimize our distinctives, yet we who have bowed before God's verbalized, propositional communication—the Bible—and before the Christ of that Bible are brothers in Christ. This we must do in the face of liberal theology. We must practice an observable and real oneness—before God, before the elect angels, before the demonic hosts, before the watching liberals and before the watching world.

appendix

some
absolute
limits

Though genuine Christians may, and in fact do, disagree over certain points of Christian thinking, there are absolute limits beyond which a Christian cannot go and still stand in the historic stream of Christianity. It will be my purpose here to discuss some of these absolute limits.

circles and cliffs

There are some Christian groups who see doctrine as being just statements of certain dogmas worded specifically according to their own terminology. If a person varies at all from this particular formulation, he is ruled out. These groups insist that there is no room for variation at all. Doctrines, even non-doctrinal intellectual positions, must be held and formulated in the exact way they dictate, and every Christian must use the exact verbalization they use.

Oftentimes if a person is raised in this kind of thinking, what occurs is that as soon as he feels in any way that he cannot subscribe to the wording as it is given, then he is severely tempted to let the pendulum swing completely away from that position. This is especially true in the case of young people and students. Not knowing that there is some freedom within the proper form, they throw Christianity away entirely. Out of such groups there is a constant stream of people who are going overboard and turning completely away from the Christian position.

To me, this is not the proper mentality. Rather, we should picture a circle within which there is freedom to move. Visualize, for example, what must have occurred on the floor of the Westminster Assembly when the Westminster Confession of Faith was being worked out. Men with varying views in regard to doctrinal detail (for example, eschatology) met together for a long time (1643-1647). What they did was to make certain statements that encompassed all the views that they agreed were faithful to the Scripture. In other words, when the Westminster Confession of Faith was framed, men with slightly different views in detail agreed that they could subscribe to this Confession. It laid down a circle in which (with their differences of doctrinal detail) they could move with freedom. The statements of the

Confession were not meant to be of a merely repetitive nature, but were meant to be a limit inside of which were those propositions which were accepted as faithful to Scripture and outside of which were those which were unacceptable in the light of Scripture. Thus there was a definite form, but within this form there was freedom for some variation.

In short, the Christian doctrinal and intellectual position lays down a circle rather than a point. Or, to say it another way, doctrines are not merely lines to be repeated. This gives freedom to express the doctrines in various ways; one is not required to repeat over and over again the same formulations in exactly the same words.

Our study here should lead us to a circle of such a nature that will warn us when we come to a place of danger. We should see the edge of the circle as an absolute limit past which we "fall off the edge of the cliff" and are no longer Christians at this particular point in our thinking. Nothing, it seems to me, could be more valuable than to recognize some of the places where the ultimate borderline rests.

Let us take, for example, a young man raised in an orthodox group who goes off to a university. He is fighting for his life, often without the lines of demarcation, the absolute limits, having been carefully laid out. He only feels vaguely, "I have to stand for this; I have to stand for that." But he does not see the real reasons for the limits; he has been given a repetitive orthodoxy, and sometimes the thing he has been taught to stand for is only a projection of the real position and not the position itself. Not knowing that he has some freedom to move within the circle, if he moves at all, everything tends to slip through his fingers.

Hence, it is tremendously important that we lay down some of these areas where in our generation we come to the edge of the cliff.

Let me first expand my analogy. With regard to the true Christian position, it seems to me that there are always two sides to the cliff, or rather, two cliffs, one on either side of the area of freedom. It is easy to fall or throw oneself over the cliff in one direction just because one is trying to escape falling off the cliff on the other side. Therefore, I want first to lay down here what seem to me to be some of the absolute limits beyond which we fall off a cliff or step outside the circle. And then I want to show, on the other hand, that there are contrary errors into which we can slide and that these throw us down the other cliff and put us equally out of the circle. If we consciously visualize these cliffs between which lie proper Christian doctrine, then I think we can see the freedom that we have to formulate, phrase and rephrase our creeds and doctrinal statements. We will see that we need not be limited to sheer memorization, and yet at the same time we will be warned before we fall off the cliff. Another way to put it is to imagine that these absolute limits are like the lens of an electric eye. When you approach one, the gong rings, you know you are in danger, and you back up.

There are at least two ways to get at these absolute limits. One way is to study the swings of the pendulum in church history. Often the church has come to a point of danger only to let the pendulum swing completely over to the opposite point of danger. The second way to get at the absolute limits is by analysis of concepts, and that will be my method here.[1]

The doctrinal areas that concern us fall into two major divisions: (1) those that comprise the intrinsic aspects of the Christian system (that is, what was as true before the Fall as it is after the Fall), and (2) those concepts that are true only after the Fall.

God and significance

We will take the intrinsic concepts first. Of these the primary concept is that God exists and that he is free.

Christianity does not have a deterministic system. We must always keep away from any sense of a deterministic system—regardless of the phrases used to state such a system. The reason that Christianity is non-deterministic is that in Christianity we have a non-determined God. This cannot be stressed too strongly. God did not create because he had to. He is "there" and he is "free," and his freedom includes

[1] With either of these two methods, a careful study of the Bible must be the basis for the limits. The bounds are set not by *any* "method" but by the truth God has given us in propositional form in the Bible.

There is one absolute limit that is crucial but which I am not dealing with in this appendix because it is dealt with in book-length detail in *He Is There and He Is Not Silent* (to be published by Hodder and Stoughton in England and Tyndale House Publishers in the United States). In this book I deal with God's "being there" *and his not being silent* in regard to propositional, verbalized communication from God to man in the areas of metaphysics (being), morals and epistemology (knowing).

the important point that he did not have to create.
Nothing can be more basic than this. Anytime you
begin to get toward the point that "God is not free,"
a little bell ought to ring.

People may very well say to you, "Well, God needs
the creation as much as the creation needs him,
because God needs to love something." Or they may
say, "God needs to be face to face with something;
God needs to be in communication with something."
But the reason that this is not so is the Trinity.
Because God is a personal God on the high order of
Trinity, God himself was everything he needed in the
area of communication and love. The persons of the
Trinity loved each other and communicated with
each other before the creation of all things. We must,
therefore, never cross this line: God exists and he did
not need to create.

There is, however, the other cliff. There is the
danger of saying that man has no significance. But
this opposite danger is met by this statement:
According to the Bible, once man has been created he
can glorify God.

The first point of the Westminster Catechism is
this: "The chief end of man is to glorify God and to
enjoy him forever." It would be scripturally false to
leave out the second phrase—"and to enjoy him
forever." The men who formulated the catechism
showed great wisdom and insight in saying, "and to
enjoy him forever." Nevertheless, the first phrase is
the first phrase: "The chief end of man is to glorify
God." And in Christianity we have a non-determined
God who did not need to create because there was

love and communication within the Trinity, and yet having been created, we as men can glorify God. That is tremendous.

But we must feel the force of both sides of the issue. If we fail to emphasize that we can glorify God, we raise the whole question of whether men are significant at all. We begin to lose our humanity as soon as we begin to lose the emphasis that what we do makes a difference. We can glorify God, and both the Old and New Testament say that we can even make God sad.

To summarize, then, the first basic absolute limit: God is free and did not need to create; yet, having been created, men though finite can glorify God— what we do makes a difference.

chance and history

The second absolute limit is related to the first: God created out of nothing, and the infinity of the Judeo-Christian, personal God is of such a nature that when he created he did not need to put chance back of himself. There is no chance back of God. This is one boundary line beyond which we fall off the cliff.

But likewise we fall off the cliff on the other side if we do not affirm that history has meaning. In Christianity cause and effect in space-time history has real meaning. The rational moral creatures whom God created (of which we know two classes—angels and men) influence history by choice. In 20th-century terms, man is not programmed. It is especially and overwhelmingly important to see that Adam was not programmed.

Even non-personal elements of God's creation have a significance in history on their own level. The wind is the cause that blows down the tree. In other words, mechanical cause and effect is significant in history, and on another level moral and rational creatures are significant in history by choice. But in one way neither is more stupendous than the other. As far as significance is concerned, the fact that the material universe that God has made has a reality of cause and effect is just as stupendous as the fact that moral, rational creatures affect history by choice. The marvel is that God created a universe with significance, that the things he created have significance.

One can say this in another way: The things God has made have a real objective existence. They are not just in the mind of God. Michelangelo's painting on the ceiling of the Sistine Chapel gives us a perfect illustration. In his painting of the creation of man, God points his finger out toward man whom he has just created. His other arm is thrown back and underneath are several figures. All but one are clearly angels (putti), but one figure stands out as different and it is clear from her breasts that she is a girl. Tradition tells us that this is Eve. Question: Is this a Christian or non-Christian painting? There is no way to tell what was in Michelangelo's mind when he painted the picture. But there are two possibilities. The first is that God knew what Eve would look like, and *therefore* even though she was not as yet created when Adam was created, she was at that time just as much in existence as she ever would be. If this is what is being pictured, it fits into Eastern thinking, but not

Christian thinking. The other possibility is that the painting simply indicates that God knew that he was going to create Eve and knew what she would look like before he created her. In this case, the concept is Christian.

The distinction is important: It made a great deal of difference to Adam whether Eve was only in the mind of God or whether an actualized, flesh and blood, beautiful Eve was before Adam as he woke from his sleep. The Bible teaches that God created things with a real, objective existence. The first corollary, then, is the objective existence of the things which God has made.

Another corollary is this: God, having created history, acts into history. It is not that history has no meaning to God; it is not as though he is suspended above it. For example, it was not the same to God before and after Jesus died on the cross (see John 7:39). And, furthermore, God does not deal with me today as if I were a 17-year-old boy, nor does he deal today with Abraham in Ur of the Chaldees. God has not put chance back of himself, and, on the other side, having created history, he truly acts into history at every given moment in such a way that he respects its being there; that is, he acts into it really, truly.

These two corollaries are just as true before the Fall as after the Fall. But there is a third corollary, relating to the second absolute limit, and it is true after the Fall but not before. That corollary is this: Since the Fall there is a work of the Holy Spirit in each man who becomes a Christian, and yet for each man there is a true conscious side to justification.

All too often the situation regarding man's salvation is discussed as an independent concept and it is forgotten that it has a place under the second basic principle, that is, that there is no chance back of God. But there is a real marvel, a real wonder that should make us worship when we realize that these things are not just intellectual or doctrinal propositions but that they are true to what is. It is really personally significant that though God did create things with true significance, yet he put no chance back of himself.

What this means since the Fall is that when man accepts Christ as Savior there has been a work of the Holy Spirit, yet man is not simply a zero; there is a conscious side to justification.

If we fail to see that there is a conscious side to justification, we soon come to the place where we must say that either the gospel is not universally offered or that man is a zero. But neither is the case. The Bible makes very plain that the gospel is universally offered and that man is significant. So if you get to the place where you begin to have scruples about the universal offer of the gospel or unless you make man a zero, you have fallen off the cliff.

Hence, it seems to me that we can equally fall off either side of the cliff. We can fall off on the side of putting chance back of God or we can fall off the cliff on the other side by denying the conscious side of justification and making man a zero.[2]

[2] The non-humanistic *basis* for a man's salvation is the infinite value of the death of Christ (as the second person of the Trinity) in space-time history on the cross. The non-humanistic *instrument* is the empty hands of faith.

unity.and diversity

The third absolute limit is this proposition: The persons of the Trinity must be kept distinct. There is true unity and diversity, not behind God but in God. This is true not just since. creation but eternally; it is true of the ontological Trinity before the creation of anything else. There is the unity of one God and yet three persons who are of such a nature that they are distinct to the extent that there is true communication and true love between the persons of the Trinity forever. As Jesus said, "the love wherein you have loved me before the creation of the world" (Jn. 17:24). Recall as well God's words in Genesis: "Let us make man in *our* own image" (Gen. 1:26). This is love and communication. It may sound simple but it is absolutely overwhelming. Everything in the Christian system rests or falls at this particular place. We must never cross this line. This is an absolute cliff, for the whole concept of personality is involved.

Furthermore, there is a total distinction between the Creator and anything created, and this distinction is absolute. In the early creeds, the church rightly understood that this distinction is to be kept even to the level of the two natures of Christ—the divine and human. This is made clear in both the Nicene and the Chalcedonian formulations—that in the person of Jesus Christ the two natures are without any confusion.

Yet if one goes too far, he falls off the cliff on the other side. For there is a unity in the person of Jesus Christ. There are two natures, but one person. It is not that one nature acts and then another nature acts, but that the person of Jesus Christ acts. This is what historic Christianity has insisted upon since the early councils, and the New Testament clearly indicates that this is so.

Yet there is another area in which one finds distinctness and yet unity. It is of *a totally different order,* but it still forms a boundary line to a circle and an edge to a cliff. On the one hand, there is an absolute distinction between the creature and the Creator, and yet there is a mystical union of the believer with Jesus Christ. I cannot say too strongly that this is of a totally *different* order than God as Trinity, but it is a line which must not be crossed, for it too forms the edge of a cliff. I would add too, that there is not only a mystical union of individual believers with Christ, but there is also a mystical union of the church with Christ. And this carries with it a further corollary: While the Bible emphasizes the value of each individual and while we must reject the overwhelming loss of this concept in modern society, the alternative is not sheer and bare individualism; there is a unity of the church as the body of Christ. In the church the individual persons who are Christians are unified as the body of Christ.

To summarize this absolute limit, one can simply say that on one side there is the cliff of confusion, and on the other side the cliff of the loss of unity. That is, on the one hand, the persons of the Trinity must be kept distinct up to the high level of love and communication between the persons of the Trinity before the creation of the world; and the Creator and creation must be kept absolutely distinct up to the level of a lack of confusion between the two natures of Christ. And on the other hand, there is the total unity of the Trinity and the total unity of the person of Jesus Christ; and there is the reality of the mystical union of the believers with Christ and the reality of unity in the body of Christ. In each of these (on very different levels), the one cliff is confusion, the other cliff is the loss of unity.

holiness and love

We come now to a fourth limit: the absolute cliff concerning the holiness of God. God has a character and his holiness is part of his character. We do not believe, as some modern theologians would have it, that God's holiness only means his being God. Rather, it means that there are some things that conform to his nature and some things that do not. God's holiness, in other words, involves moral content.

Modern theologians are apt to take holiness as just meaning God's metaphysical otherness. But this is not what the Bible teaches. The biblical God is not Tillich's god, god behind God; and he is not a god who is everything and therefore nothing. To repeat: There are those moral actions which conform to God's character and those that do not.

Of course, this has tremendous ramifications, for the fact that God is holy means something to the individual and it means something to the group. It demands holiness in our personal life and holiness in the church in both life and doctrine. All these stand not as isolated factors, but together upon the reality that God is holy.

And yet we must immediately respond that we fall off the opposite cliff if we forget that God is love. There is a great emphasis on love today. It is often viewed as having almost no direction, as being an unmotivated love—love that is to be equal in all directions. But God's love is not contentless or directionless for the simple reason that God does not "lack content." He has a character. The great statements of truth in the Bible, the great doctrines and the law of God—these lay down the tracks for love. We can, therefore, fall into heresy in two ways. We can forget either God's holiness or his love, and we cannot say which of these is worse.

We must realize that love alone is not the end of the matter. It rests upon the character of God and God is the God who is Holy and the God who is Love. We would not choose between love and holiness, for to forget either is equally vicious. But we do have to realize that the talk of love we are so surrounded by today is often a love without tracks. Therefore, when we begin to deal in practice with God's holiness, we must always remember that simultaneously there must be the reality of love. And when we begin to deal in practice with God's love, we must remember that simultaneously there must be the reality of his holiness. It is not that we do one and then the other, like keeping a ball in the air with two ping-pong paddles. Both God's holiness and his love must be exhibited simultaneously or we have fallen off one cliff or the other.

This doctrine is very practical. It relates not only

to our intellectual and doctrinal thinking, but to our practice as individuals and groups. For true love will always produce true holiness both in doctrine and in life. And, on the other hand, true holiness will always produce love both in doctrine and in life. All of this is true, I say again, because neither love nor holiness hangs in midair; they both rest upon the character of the God who is there, the God who is holy and the God who is love. And we are called upon to exhibit his existence and his character at every moment of our lives.

objectivity and subjectivity of history

We come now to the second major classification. All of those absolute limits that I have discussed above (with the exception of one corollary) have been intrinsic, that is, they are as true before the Fall as after the Fall. I now come to those absolute limits which are true only after the Fall, which are related to the abnormality of the universe since the Fall. The first absolute limit under this category is this: the historic space-time nature of the Fall.

Words have become so devalued today that we often have to use cumbersome terms to make what we mean understood. The word *fact* does not necessarily mean anything anymore. *Fact* can just mean upper-story religious truth, and therefore we have to use an awkward term like *brute fact*. In this particular case, we are fortunate because the liberal theologians themselves use the term *brute fact* for what *they don't* mean by facts. At least for the time being we have a term that we can agree on. Orthodox

Christians, for example, believe in the *brute fact* of the historic, space-time Fall. The historic Fall is not an interpretation; it is a *brute fact*. There is no room for hermeneutics here, if by heremeneutics we mean explaining away the *brute factness* of the Fall. That there was a Fall is not an upper-story statement—that is, it is not in this sense a "theological" or "religious" statement. Rather it is a historic, space-time, *brute fact*, propositional statement.

Furthermore, as a result of this historic, space-time Fall the world is no longer the way it was when God made it, and the change came as a result of the historic Fall. To say it another way, there was a time before the Fall when the world was not abnormal but normal. The denial of this concept is like a greased plank. The grease on the plank is any temptation to forget even for a wavering moment the abnormality of the present universe.

Rationalistic philosophy and theology begin with the concept of the normality of the world.[3] The rationalist begins with himself and with the world around him and assumes that what he sees is representative of the normal state of affairs. But this is not the case. The Christian thinker begins with the infinite-personal God who created the world (a normal world), and then he recognizes the fact that after the historic, space-time Fall, the world became abnormal.

Likewise, Christ's death and resurrection are historic, space-time *brute facts* that have already oc-

[3]The later Heidegger did show that he at least felt a problem here in that he brought in the concept of epistemological abnormality with Aristotle. See *The God Who Is There*, p. 185.

curred, and the second coming of Christ is a historic, space-time *brute fact* that will occur in the future. What a contrast to neo-orthodox eschatology which does not refer to future space-time history, but to present, here-and-now purpose! There is no compromise at this point: Either these things are space-time *brute facts* or they aren't.

One should wake up in the night saying to himself, "We live in an abnormal universe!" All of what we write, teach, preach and discuss should be grounded in the realization that the Fall, Christ's death, his resurrection and his second coming are propositional; they are *brute facts.*

We can carry this further. If we are children of God, there was a historic, space-time moment when we passed from death to life; there was a historic, space-time moment when God as judge declared us individually justified, a moment when God declared that our true moral guilt was forgiven on the basis of the finished work of Jesus Christ in history. Furthermore, there will be a historic future complete salvation at the coming of the Lord Jesus, the resurrection of the body and the redemption of creation. When we do not affirm these things, then we fall off the cliff on one side.

But there is another cliff that we can fall off just as easily. We do so, if we fail to stress that these things are not *only* bare doctrines, *only* bare propositions or *bare* facts. These *brute facts* have meaning in the present. All of the past, present and future historic events that we have insisted were *brute facts* have a present meaning in the history of our own lives.

Christ's death has a present meaning in history at this moment in my life; so does his resurrection. To put it another way, we must reject the concept of subjectivity with regard to these historical events, but we must also realize that these *brute facts* are not just abstractions or bare propositions. They are to have meaning in our present life, and they are to be acted upon in our present lives. There is no Christian doctrine that does not have meaning in the existential, moment-by-moment life. For example, the doctrine of the Trinity is affirmed in our Christian lives as we practice the reality and the importance of personality at this present moment. This is true both in the practice of personal relationship toward God and toward people.

Jesus' first commandment is to "love the Lord your God with all your heart and soul and mind." And the second commandment is like it, "to love your neighbor as yourself." The emphasis in our generation is on subjective "religious truth," and this is our great enemy. But it is also true that in the midst of fighting this enemy it is possible to back off the other side of the cliff, to think of these things only as dogmas, only as creeds, only as bare propositions and to forget that they have a personal aspect as well. The end of the matter is not the bare dogma; it is the propositional, true knowledge that has the result of our loving the Lord with all our heart and our neighbors as ourselves in our present moment-by-moment lives.

justification and sanctification

Let us now look at a second absolute limit that falls

under the category of those things which are true after the Fall. Mistakes at this point do not rule out a person's being a Christian, but such mistakes do conflict with biblical lines and open the door to serious confusion. Justification must not be confused with sanctification. Again there are two sides to the absolute limit: Justification is once-for-all; and this justification is not to be confused with the moment-by-moment Christian life. Justification is once-for-all and yet if there are no signs of such a moment-by-moment Christian life, we must question whether or not there has ever been justification.

Similarly within the area of sanctification: Sanctification is a process and not an act. Yet there is often a crisis, at least in the sense of new knowledge that we are then called to act upon. Many people who do not fall off the cliff on the side of making sanctification a once-for-all act fall off the cliff by thinking and acting as though one is justified and sanctified by an automatic, unconscious process. Sanctification is a process, but it is not a mechanical process in which the Christian takes no conscious part. Very often there is a crisis in a Christian's life when he is told or when he learns for himself from Scripture what the work and the death of Christ can mean to his moment-by-moment life, and he begins to act on this.

Related to this is the fact that it is fruitless to argue whether a Christian can be free from all known sin at any one moment. This is so for the simple reason that since the Fall, we are complex people—very complex people—and each man is divided from himself. The whole question of complete victory at any one moment is foolish in the light of the way we fool ourselves deep into our own subconscious being. Since the Fall, we lie to ourselves, and none of us is capable of knowing fully what is known and what is not known to ourselves.

At the same time, we can fall off the opposite cliff by failing to put sufficient emphasis on the Bible's call for a sinless life. The command is clear as a bell: no second-rate standards. "Be perfect as your Father in heaven is perfect." In his fight against the concept of a static perfectionism, the careful theologian will insist that we sin daily in thought, word and deed. But woe betide us if we count this our norm. That is totally destructive. There is a difference between the declarative statement that we sin daily and the normative statement that such sinning is acceptable. We can say that we sin daily in thought, word and deed without then resting upon our oars and excusing ourselves. Again, to go over either side of the cliff is equally destructive.

We can summarize these points this way: (1) Justification is once-for-all, and yet, if there is no Christian life, one must ask whether a man has been justified; (2) Sanctification is a process, not an act, and yet there are often one or more crises along the way as a Christian gains new knowledge of the meaning and the work of Christ in his present life and as he begins to act on that knowledge; (3) It is fruitless to discuss the question of whether we can have victory over all known sin, and yet we cannot let this become normative in the sense of forgetting that the standard is perfection. Put it this way: Can you imagine the God of perfection, light and beauty saying, "Just sin a little bit"? As soon as we say it, we know it is false.

absolute right and wrong

Finally, we come to the last absolute limit that I wish to deal with: There is such a thing as absolute right and absolute wrong in systems. Of course, in our generation the whole direction is toward being unwilling to say that any system is right or wrong. Even many who consider themselves evangelicals are embarrassed by the Reformers' saying that the Roman Catholic system as a system was wrong. But we must affirm the possibility of right and wrong with regard to systems and categories. We fall off the cliff on one side if we do not do so.

But there is another side to the cliff: None of us is completely consistent in our Christian thinking. We must declare non-Christian systems false. And furthermore we must declare as true the Christian system which begins with the existence of the infinite-personal God on the high order of the Trinity—a God who created all that now exists (except himself, who has always been) and who can and does act into the universe he has made and who gives propositional knowledge in verbalized form to man. And yet, we must understand that none of us is totally consistent in presenting the Christian system.

The Reformers expressed an important concept, namely, that although there are true churches and false churches, in the area of true churches, there are those that are more and those that are less pure. The same thing, I suggest, is true not only of churches but of the expression of Christian teaching. We must be careful not to see everything as relative, some systems being 90%, some systems being 59%, etc. For this is not so. Lines are crossed when churches and systems pass from the things that are true to those that are false. Yet, we must not fall off the other cliff by thinking that any of us expresses the Christian teaching in a completely perfect fashion. Since the Fall we are not perfect in our bodies; our bodies are yet to be raised from the dead. We are not perfect in our sanctification; our sanctification is yet to be completed. And we are not totally consistent in our expression of the Christian teaching either. Yet we must not fall off the cliff in failing to stress that everything is not relative. There is such a thing as a right and wrong in systems.

This balance keeps us from a sectarian way of thinking; it keeps us from chewing up everyone who differs with us on any point of Christian doctrine. This is a very practical cliff indeed. For example, some of us have experienced sending our children to a university town away from home. What are we to say to them then? Certainly we must not say, "Well, after all, it doesn't matter where you go to church; it's just a matter of averages anyway so it doesn't matter." But neither should we say, "You've got to find a perfect church before you can go to it." Putting it more personally, what do I say? Do I say, "You have to find a church that agrees down to every last detail with what I teach"? That's ridiculous. Nor do I say, "It doesn't matter where you go." What I say is,

"Find a Bible-believing church and go there." This is not to say that one is going to agree with every detail that is taught, nor is it to say that there is no time or place to discuss our Christian distinctives. There is that which within the true circle is more or less pure according to our own light as we study the Scripture. But if a church is a Bible-believing church, it falls in the circle and you are not falling off the cliff. If it is a true church, we may send our children with quietness of mind. The same advice applies to Christian converts as well.

form and freedom inside the circle

I wish to conclude by summarizing. Christianity is not to be considered as a single point or a narrow, repetitive line, but as a circle which provides form but within which there is freedom to move in terms of understanding and expression. Christianity is a circle with definite limits, limits which tend to be like twin cliffs. We find ourselves in danger of falling off on one side or on the other; that is, we have to be careful not to avoid one sort of doctrinal error by backing off into the opposite one.

We must ask God to help us, and we must help each other, not to fall off the cliffs. There is room for discussion within each circle, but we must not forget that there is a circle to be in.